This book should be read with the understanding that the author is not engaged in rendering legal advice. If legal advice is required, the services of an attorney should be sought. No warranties are expressed or implied.

Published by:
ServiceWinners International Sdn. Bhd.
No. 3-33, Jalan Puteri 4/8
Bandar Puteri
47100 Puchong
Selangor DE, Malaysia
Website: http://www.servicewinners.com

Perpustakaan Negara Malaysia   Cataloguing-in-Publication Data
Coyle, Steven F., 1959-
   Good Boss, Better Boss: practical leadership models for post-Covid
   success / Steven F.
   Coyle.—First Edition 2021.
   ISBN: 978-967-19831-1-9
   1. Supervisors.
   2. Leadership.
   3. Executives.
   I. Title.
   658.302

Design & prepress by: HMDpublishing.com
Edited by: Augustine Chay

Seminars we offer:

• Good Boss, Better Boss	• Coaching & Calibration Skills
• First Steps in Management	• Influencing & Negotiation Skills
• Winning Collection Skills	• Handling Hardcore Debtors
• Handling Hardcore Customers	• Winning Service Skills
• Train-the-Trainer (TTT) Skills	• Success Begins with Me!
• Retail Selling Skills	• Business Writing & Case Writing Skills
• Winning Telesales Skills	• Ethics @ Work

ServiceWinners International Sdn. Bhd.

"Changing the world, one better boss after another"

Steven Coyle

Tel: +60 12-2000-998

E-Mail : steve@servicewinners.com

Website: www.servicewinners.com

Note: While I draw from many first-hand experiences, the names of colleagues, clients, supervisees, and mentees have changed to protect their privacy.

In this book, the words "leader" and "supervisor" are used interchangeably. If you see either of these two words, the other is implied.

Supervisors, Leaders, Managers, CEOs. Have you ever wondered….?

- How to motivate and lead your teams to higher results?

- What practical, easy models to use with your people?

- How to raise your department's exposure to reflect the importance of what you do?

- How to increase your organizational value to move upward and onward?

- How to communicate, lead, and motivate your team post-COVID?

- How to attract and retain top performers to win the talent war?

This book answers these questions and more. It's full of creative, PRACTICAL ideas and models to ensure you lead well. The author shares tips learned in the West and East to lead successful multi-ethnic teams during stormy, post-COVID seas.

If you're:

- a supervisor

- a manager

- a CEO (or 'C' anything)

- a military officer

- a government director

- a professional

- a business owner

- a politician

- or anyone who leads others or will lead others one day

The book's practical and easy models will help you become a better leader and achieve better results.

GOOD BOSS, BETTER BOSS

Practical Leadership Models for
Post-COVID Success

Steven F. Coyle

To COVID-19,
Without you this book would
never have been written.

Contents

Chapter 6.

Chapter 7.

PREFACE

As a supervisor, I often needed quick, practical ideas from others in the field of supervision. Sometimes I turned to books, but most were written by academics and consultants who did little if any supervising or leading teams. This practical book is geared for people who lead and supervise others on a daily basis. I share many easy-to-remember, time-saving models that you can use while putting out your day-to-day supervisory fires.

This book focuses on the most difficult parts of your job: communicating and managing people. It also covers how to succeed in your organization by moving yourself upwards and onwards. You will gain new techniques on successfully dealing with your peers, boss, senior management, suppliers, customers, and even competitors to increase your organizational value.

I have led large and small teams and together we have experienced success and sometimes failure. I will share my experiences to make you a better supervisor and leader. I'm lucky to have worked with some great teams and bosses. I've also worked with a few horrible bosses, but the horrible ones have taught me what not to do. I do believe that all of us can become **better** bosses.

If you have any comments, techniques, or questions about the art of leading people, please feel free to contact me.

Terima kasih,

Steve Coyle

ServiceWinners International Sdn. Bhd.

Kuala Lumpur, Malaysia

Phone: +60-12-2000-998

Email: steve@servicewinners.com

Website: www.servicewinners.com

ACKNOWLEDGEMENTS

I would like to thank my editor, Augustine Chay, for his in-depth critiques and professionalism. I'm also grateful to business practitioners (i.e., living examples of great bosses) who have made a major impact on my life's work.

They are:

Australia: Andrew Gan

Canada: Alexander Montagano and Tim Paulsen

Germany: Daniel Ord

Laos: Anthony Chin

Malaysia: Albert Khoo, Barry Spencer, Jude Louis, Sasheedran Raman, Peter Butler, Adzhar Ibrahim, Nora Manaf, Cabrini Lee Lay Wun, Tay Yow Hong, Tham Mon Li, Farid Reizal Anual, Khalipah Mastura Abd Rahim, Suhana Abd. Rahim, Mohd Huzaini Hamdi, Christina Yap, Santhi Sukumaran, Kiang Chew Peng, Azmi Ujang, and Kue Kit Man.

Poland: Pawel Miller

Thailand: Dean Hughson

United States of America: Steve Akrish, Michael Kinneman, DeDe Herbert, Colleen Cowhick, Nick and Marianne Boechler, Tom Hehir, Rene Villa, Doug Faber, Charlie Klever, J. Kirby Pain, David T. Payne, Ronald L. Riecks, Brooks Berry, Tom Magrath, and Elizabeth C. Coyle.

GOOD BOSS, BETTER BOSS

Practical Leadership Models for Post-COVID Success

Steven F. Coyle

INTRODUCTION

You're reading this book because either you want to be a better leader or supervisor — or you're buying it for someone who is or will be a leader or supervisor. Most books on leadership and supervisory skills are too theoretical for me. They are written by 'experts' who make more money as experts than as leaders and supervisors.

In this book I've shared many examples, techniques, and models that led to most of my staff calling me a good boss. Of course, a few supervisees have called me a bad boss (or worse). Supervisors can't please everyone, but if your poor performers—who remained poor after your intervention—still call you a bad boss, that's great. They're bad employees.

But, if your top performers call you a bad boss, then you are bad. Your situation is dire. You MUST immediately change your style, techniques, and attitude or you will be fired. Your top performers, to your organization, are more valuable than you because they deliver the results.

My work experience is in the banking, telecommunication, and education fields in the U.S., Poland, and Malaysia. Since 2003 I have led a Malaysian-based consultancy team that takes on assignments around the world. I have lived, worked, and travelled to 40 countries. Along the way, I have worked with some great organizations and teams comprised of diverse ethnicities.

The techniques in this book apply from the lowest front-line supervisors to 'C' level senior employees. We all supervise no matter our job title. I'm a corporate trainer and many of my models use mnemonics to make them easier to remember.

Let me be upfront: I am apprehensive when I hear the word 'leader.' When that word hits my ears, I immediately think of either senior management or senior politicians. In most cases they have disappointed me. When I hear the word 'coach', my feelings are more positive as coaches — in my life — have cared more for me than leaders. When I hear the word 'supervisor', I get a taste in my mouth akin to vegetables. Critically important to our well-being, but sometimes not so tasty.

Perhaps because I live in Asia, I prefer the word, "boss", and I use it a lot in this book.

My Senior Management Story 

When I was a low-level employee at a U.S. wireless telecom operator, my employer was bought out by a larger competitor. My colleagues and I were all nervous about the new ownership change. My employer bused all its employees to a cinema to explain how the merger would affect our jobs. Our CEO had Hollywood looks and was dressed in cool high-tech style: unbuttoned suit jacket, no tie, loafers, and perfect, jet-black hair.

At the end of his presentation, he opened the floor to questions.

One of us asked, "Jim, will you be coming with us into the new venture?"

He replied, "Yes." The whole cinema erupted with applause. We gave him a standing ovation.

Two weeks later he resigned to launch his start-up company. He must have been planning this for months, maybe even years.

When I see people standing to applaud leaders, I think of all the bad things that can happen (from a historical standpoint). I'm not keen about people calling themselves 'leaders', as really, they are just humans with their own strengths and weaknesses. In any organization, leaders are merely employees at a higher salary grade and position than others. As humans, their #1 goal isn't the company, or you, but their own lives and families. You can't blame them. You would have done the same.

Still, we humans like to put other humans on pedestals. So why not take advantage of leadership opportunities? You can earn more money and recognition. You can gain new skills and contacts. You will become more valuable.

Each leader is a supervisor. Each supervisor is a leader. The only difference is in salary, power, and influence. The jobs are the same — just on different scales. Of course, some bosses are better than others.

Yet although supervisors and leaders are essentially the same, the word 'leadership' has become a buzzword in today's management thinking. I've spent a large portion of my working life in the corporate training world. I know that the trainers who make the most money specialize in 'leadership training.'

Whatever that is?

My Leadership Training Story

My training partner and friend, Jude Louis, invited me to a networking event hosted by the Australian embassy here in Kuala Lumpur, Malaysia. The venue was at a nice lodge in a jungle outside of KL. It was a trainers-meet-trainers event. A delegation of Australian-based trainers was brought to meet and network with Malaysian trainers.

Although the embassy had the best of intentions, I immediately knew that this would be a waste of time. Trainers are lone wolves. They don't work well together. It should have been an event where Australian trainers met Malaysian corporate training managers. Corporate training managers aren't lone wolves. They are employees who have access to a company's training budget. They have the power to hire trainers. Anyway, since Jude is a good friend, I went.

The venue and the food were wonderful. Since it was an Australian event, there was plenty of booze. When their training delegation arrived, it was as if a convention of Barbie and Ken dolls had arrived. They were gorgeous. Their teeth so white. Their hair so perfect. Their clothes so dashing. The men reminded me of televangelists. No one seemed to be over 45. Whereas I was 55, overweight, and nearly bald.

There were ten of them and as I met each one, I asked, "So what kind of training do you do?" Each answered, "Leadership." But their responses varied when I asked, "What kind of leadership training do you do?"

Some said teambuilding skills, others leadership values, others grooming skills, others presentation skills, others gave nebulous responses as if they were trying to describe heaven, "To build a non-threatening culture of empowerment and inspiration to meet organizational targets." But I wondered, aren't good supervisors supposed to do all these?

When they asked me what kind of training I did? I said, "Supervisory skills." Maybe it was my insecurity in facing such beautiful people, but I could have sworn they responded with the word, "Oh." Then looked at me as if they felt sorry for me, like, 'Oh, I remember when I was in this guy's shoes, poor fella.' Although the event was fun (what event isn't fun with free food and drinks?), it was non-productive. It resulted in no new business or novel insights about 'leadership.'

To keep this book small, I'm focusing on the more artistic—and more difficult—aspects of supervising others. I share models, tips, ideas, and experiences. The book's goal is to help you become a better leader, supervisor, commander, manager, CEO, or whatever job title you have. How will you become a better boss? You will do that by strengthening your communication skills, getting the right people on your team, coaching correctly, and—most importantly—building the right work environment to deliver the results. Today, COVID-19 has given us an added challenge. Although some parts of a supervisor's job are timeless, the pandemic has clearly disrupted many aspects.

Let me briefly explain the book's nine chapters:

Chapter 1: What Exactly is Good Leadership?

My idea of good leadership is probably different from yours. In this chapter, I explain the two qualities that good leaders must possess. You either have them by now or you don't.

For the purposes of the book, I assume you possess these two qualities.

Chapter 2: Who Are You? Who Are They?

We start by understanding ourselves and other people's four main types of personalities to connect with others (and ourselves). By understanding others' personalities, we will have an easier time connecting and influencing them to achieve the desired results.

Chapter 3: Building the Right Systems and Processes

Like in nature, how people live and work is dependent on their environment. It's important to implement the right systems and processes in order to create a performance-based, creative, pleasant work environment that reflects yours, theirs, and your organization's values. If you create the wrong work environment, you will fail.

Chapter 4: Communication

Humans are social, communicative beings. Your success as a supervisor depends on how you communicate with others at all levels. E.g., your subordinates, peers, superiors, investors, Board, and customers. Working hard isn't enough. Being smart isn't enough. Your communication skills will help you lead your team to achieve the result. Good communication skills also get you hired and promoted.

Chapter 5: Managing People

Supervising is one of our most difficult tasks as most people don't like to be told what to do. We will cover how to get maximum results out of your people while building a motivational work environment, especially post-COVID.

Chapter 6: Coaching

People are sensitive when receiving feedback and this chapter focuses on how to give feedback to continue 'good' behaviors and change 'bad' behaviors. I will share my 5-Step 'House Model'. A supervisor who gives feedback incorrectly kills team synergy and motivation. It's critical that you master this skill well to avoid harming your people.

Chapter 7: Handling Problems

A large portion of our day is spent putting out fires, handling complaints, and problem-solving. It's easy leading people when the 'seas are calm.' But supervising during stormy weather shows you and your people whether you are a true leader or not.

Chapter 8: Preparing For Your Next Act

We focus on helping you move upwards and onwards in your career.

Chapter 9: 7 Common Supervisory Questions with Answers

Quick responses to questions and problems many supervisors have.

I hope you find my book useful. I wish you all the best in your quest to improve yourself, become a better boss, and enjoy the rewards.

We can always become better at what we do, especially in this new post-COVID world.

CHAPTER 1

WHAT EXACTLY IS LEADERSHIP?

"A leader is one who knows the way, goes the way, and shows the way."
– John C. Maxwell, American leadership
expert, author, and speaker

Everybody wants to be a leader nowadays. And why not? Leaders get more recognition and pay. Leadership trainers get paid a lot of money. People who run leadership conventions can become millionaires. Humans crave leaders, but we don't like bosses.

How do you define a leader?

Some academics and training institutes have delineated multiple leadership competencies in an attempt to reduce leadership to a science. They promise that mastery of these 47 competencies will make you a bona fide leader. Some universities even offer PhD degrees in leadership. Doesn't this make you wonder if most of the world's leaders ever received a leadership degree?

To me, there are only two qualities that make you a good leader. And you either have them by now or you don't. These two qualities must be developed at an early stage in your life. And only you will know whether you possess them. In fact, you don't even need to supervise or lead others (except yourself) to cultivate these qualities.

I DON'T believe that you can drill leadership skills into adults. If you can't lead as a young adult, even if it's just yourself, then how can a mere workshop or course make up *all* the difference? Greta Thunberg, the Swedish climate change activist, started her worldwide campaign at age 16. She exemplifies how youth is not incompatible with good leadership. Whereas certain old world leaders, to me, aren't good leaders.

Leadership isn't about skills (that's in the domain of supervision); leadership is about the inherent beliefs and strengths that you developed long before you started working. These qualities aren't simply acquired through a class, a few books, or a convention. You can't be trained to be a leader, but you can be trained to be a better leader.

Most 'leadership training' is a con job, akin to looking for water with a divining stick. It's hocus-pocus, kumbaya, feel good stuff that puffs up your ego and fades soon after the 'training' ends. An easy way to discern this is by asking 'leadership training' participants two questions:

1) "How was it?"

They usually respond with "great"; "fun"; "the best training in my life."

2) "What did you learn?"

There is an uncomfortable silence. The higher the price the organization paid for the leadership training, the more uncomfortable the silence.

Let's face it: leadership is getting others to support or follow you to achieve the desired results. To get people to follow you, you use a mixture of influencing and negotiation techniques alongside a combination of carrots and sticks. Since I want to be a 'good' leader, my repertoire places less emphasis on fear, intimidation, and punishment — while favoring rewards, encouragement, and positive reinforcement. Fear works, but only to a certain level. To outcompete other teams and companies, you need more than fear. Respect works wonders.

I nevertheless support the use of a little fear. Fear doesn't need to have a horribly negative connotation. A little fear is good. You just need to channel it towards positive outcomes. A total lack of fear breeds complacency.

There are two essential characteristics of a good leader. If you lack one, you'll never successfully lead others over a long period of time. No amount of classroom time, leadership conventions, scholarly research, or 'character-building' activities will endow you with these two qualities.

They are:

1. Courage (this is most important)

2. Ethics

Any other important leadership characteristics are not characteristics but competencies — anyone can learn them.

This is the bottom line: If you need someone to tell you or teach you how to be a leader, then you're not one. Most leadership training isn't about leadership training; it's about supervisory training, self-development, or rah-rah teambuilding. The question isn't: Are you a leader? You already know the answer. The question is: Should you lead others?

To my young readers: Don't worry if you haven't had a chance to lead others yet. If you're courageous and ethical, your time will come. The cream rises to the top. In the meantime, take on more responsibilities to increase your successes or failures, both will increase your self-confidence and courage.

1. Courage

Do you believe in yourself? Do you take reasonable risks? Do you accept the blame for your decisions (and those made by your people) when things go wrong? Do you address problems immediately? Do you address the problems caused by senior management to prevent them from adversely affecting your people and your department? Do you tell the truth? Are you courageous enough to be open-minded and **change your decision if another person's insight is better?** Do you highlight organizational injustices? Do you stand up for your team to customers, peers, and senior management?

Courage is the most critical prerequisite for good leadership. You can be a leader without ethics, but you can't be an ethical leader without courage. Is it even ethical to lack the courage you need to confront injustice? If you lack courage, eventually, others will see you crumble.

During a particular Southeast Asian work project, the Head of HR asked me to write a non-discrimination policy for their organization. The policy would be discussed at their next HR leadership meeting. At the meeting, the leader saw that my policy included gender as a non-discrimination factor. He asked me to take it out. I argued the non-discrimination policies of most modern companies include gender. He still insisted. I looked around the conference table for support from my fellow HR leaders, but none of them made eye contact. Since half the attendees were women, this was especially disheartening. Despite their high salaries and relatively prestigious job titles, they weren't leaders.

By 'courage' I don't mean stupid or false courage. This type of courage causes rash decisions that often backfire. A leader who makes too many rash decisions with stupid or false courage will eventually be replaced.

I've found leaders with courage but no ethics. Peter Drucker, the father of management thinking and a witness to Hitler's rise to power, calls such individuals 'mis-leaders'[1]. Most dictators leave a legacy that is heavy in blood but light on collective progress. Sure, they had courage and often unpar-

---

1   Rich Karlgaard, "Peter Drucker on Leadership," Forbes, November 19, 2004, https://www.forbes.com/2004/11/19/cz_rk_1119drucker.html#52fc2c096f48 (Accessed 6 January 2021). Drucker warns about the dangers of charismatic leadership in the interview.

alleled charisma, but they used any means available to maintain their power and pursue their objectives.

On the other hand, leaders with ethics but no courage are cowards. History forgets many of them as their impact is often minimal. If you lead without courage, your performance will reflect your fearful disposition to your team, peers, boss, senior management, board of directors, and customers. You are unwittingly getting yourself fired.

Since leaders are paid more, they need to demonstrate their added value by displaying courage. Unfortunately, I've found many leaders to be so desperate to cover their ass that they become gutless.

When I was working for an American finance company, I was forced to sit in on my boss' call with our home office in New York. New York was calling because my colleague, Roger, a good performer, forgot to file a legal document. This honest mistake could potentially cause a million-dollar loss if the customer defaulted on its loan. Roger and I listened to our boss mention Roger's name and emphasize how sorry Roger was for the mistake. Although I personally liked my boss and considered him an ethical leader, he was a coward. I wanted to rip the phone from his hands and have Roger explain the situation himself since our boss wasn't defending him.

2. Ethics

Are you a good person? Will you lie, cheat, and steal to achieve your target? Do you put yourself or your position ahead of the good of your people or organization? Will you burn down bridges, villages, and people to get what you want (the ends justify the means)? Do people trust you? Do you set a good example? Are you fair? Are you on the take? Are you prejudiced-based or performance-based when evaluating your team members?

Pawel Miller, a CEO based in Poland, had to help a formerly communist or socialist state-run company transition to a private, capitalist structure. He said that the hardest part of the transition was tackling peoples' entrenched mindsets.

To lead this change, he firmly believes in the importance of authenticity:

> I couldn't promise them much except sweat and blood. The journey was going to be tough. I ended up laying off 65% of the workforce, but I told the survivors that the distant future will be bright. And it was. We were able to stem the losses after four years; whereas the new owners expected it to take five years to turn it around. In fact, some of the retrenched staff even contacted me to say 'thank you' for retrenching them. They said, although painful at the time, the retrenchment helped them learn new skills and better prepare for work in a capitalistic environment.

Humans are imperfect creatures. Our courage and ethics are on a continuum. The best, most inspirational, and wisest leaders are at the higher ends of the spectrum. The SOBs, dictators, despots, psychopaths, cowards and criminals ('misleaders') are at the lower ends.

Our lives are governed by ethical principles. In today's IT age these principles could be called our 'operating system' (O/S). Is your O/S an ethical one? Whether it is or isn't WILL affect the type of leader you are. If you are an unethical, back-stabbing subordinate; you will become an unethical, back-stabbing leader. You can't simply change your character. It has taken you years to develop, test, and perfect your O/S.

Humans, like apes, respect dominance and confidence. Strongmen appeal to us. Many of them rise up in the corporate world, but that doesn't mean they are good leaders. They lead with fear and charisma, not ethics.

Only you will know if you are courageous and ethical. If you are, you can become a great supervisor. If you aren't, you can still be a leader and supervisor—but I feel sorry for your subordinates. We extol leaders who demonstrate both qualities because they left the world a better place. This includes individuals like Nelson Mandela, George Washington, Angela Merkel, Bill Gates, and hopefully, you.

If your courage levels are low, you can do something about it. You can push yourself into challenging experiences that test yourself. I find the more challenging situations the better. Overcoming challenging circumstances- and sometimes even failing in them—leads to increased courage as most people avoid challenges. Create a support system of people who share your ethics that you can rely on when taking courageous decisions. These people can be family, friends, mentors, key team members, senior bosses, board members—even God.

Your job gives you power, influence, and the ability to change people's lives. How well you use it determines how well your people remember you. Your courage and ethics will determine if you become a memorable boss. Headhunters advise their job-seeking clients to pay the most attention to who their future supervisor will be if they take up a new position in a different company. If he or she is a good boss, the new job can be wonderful because good bosses develop you into something you never knew you could become.

I see this in the careers of top athletes. Some will give up more lucrative offers because they want to play for a certain coach. The coach has a winning track record and is known for developing his or her players. Who doesn't want to win? Who doesn't want to be developed into the best that s/he can be? Great coaches are a key factor in attracting great talent. This factor isn't limited to the world of professional sports.

Good bosses help people win and exceed their limitations. Bad bosses, well...

For the sake of simplicity, I will minimize using the word 'leader' throughout the rest of this book— 'supervisor' or 'boss' will be privileged instead. For me, the word 'leader' is loaded with too many misconceptions and falsehoods. Too many management theorists put leaders on pedestals while belittling those who manage or supervise. In reality, leaders manage and supervise — while managers and supervisors also lead.

My Chapter's Key Points:

- Leadership comes down to two characteristics: 1) courage; 2) ethics. You either have them by now or you don't. Of the two, courage is the more important one.

Provided you have the characteristics of a leader, the next chapter focuses on connecting with the different types of people you will lead.

CHAPTER 2

WHO ARE YOU? WHO ARE THEY?

People often say that this or that person has not yet found himself. But the self is not something one finds; it is something one creates.
– Thomas Szasz, Hungarian-American psychiatrist and academic

In life, we devote a lot of time trying to understand who we really are. I have tried to discover who I am all my life.

This drive manifested itself in my travels. After college in Washington state, I moved to Alaska and worked as a banker. I helped companies finance their industrial assets: trucks, construction equipment, and fishing vessels.

I eventually left Alaska to travel the world. Over the span of 1.5 years, I worked on a kibbutz, saw the Middle East, Western Europe, and North Africa. I rode in a date truck across the Sahara Desert to see West Africa.

After that, I returned to the U.S. and joined the telecommunications industry as a debt collector and customer service agent.

The travel bug took hold of me again and I moved to Poland for two years, where I worked as an English teacher right after the Berlin Wall collapsed. I witnessed the gut-wrenching changes the Polish people experienced as their nation transitioned from a communist state with a planned economy to a liberal state with a capitalist system. The biggest changes they endured were the mental ones. They suddenly needed to learn how to survive with using their own skills and knowledge.

I returned to the U.S. and re-joined my former telecommunications employer. I transitioned into the role of a corporate trainer. In 1995, they sent me to their Malaysian joint-venture to start up a new telecommunications company. I worked in their Customer Service and HR training departments in Kuala Lumpur. I married my Malaysian colleague.

In 2003, my wife and I started ServiceWinners International: a Malaysian-based training and consultancy company. This entrepreneurial spirit has taken me to Brunei, Thailand, Indonesia, Myanmar, Singapore, India, Afghanistan, and Cyprus.

I am now 61 years old. I can speak French, some Malay, and some Polish. I still don't know who I am. I do know what I like and dislike. I know what I'm good and not good at. We are all unfinished works of art. Throughout our lives we may polish up our canvas a bit, but at the end, we're still just an unfinished canvas.

Like most young people, I wanted to learn more about myself. But can we fully understand ourselves when we accumulate our unique prejudices, blind spots, and insecurities? As we grow older, hopefully some of those insecurities decrease in intensity — allowing us to be confident enough to accept our weaknesses.

When I was young, I had a hard time taking criticism — especially incorrect or badly delivered criticism. As I matured, it became easier but never effortless. Humans are sensitive creatures, both physically and emotionally.

Scientists claim that the largest organ in the human body is our skin. We are a watery mess of blood and organs, held upright by a few bones, and encapsulated with meters of sensitive skin. We are a walking pin cushion. As a boss, you will need to be aware of this as you will be giving orders, feedback, and bad news to people who are overloaded with feelings. In a post-COVID context, there is a pivot to remote-based workers, flexi-hours, and economic instability and we will need to put extra effort in getting to know our team members and their diverse personalities.

It's OK if you don't understand yourself fully. We all don't. But it's important to be honest to yourself about what you are good at and not good at. We may be able to narrow some gaps in our weaknesses, but for some others—never. We need a strategy on how to handle those skill gaps. Will it be to delegate that deficit in expertise to someone else? Or to ask a colleague for help? Or to hire a new person? Or to ask your boss for assistance? You will need to deal with it, one way or another, to be successful.

One of my many deficits is a lack of attention to detail. It seems many job descriptions require the candidate to be a 'strategic thinker' and 'detailed oriented.' These skills are often mutually exclusive. The folks who can think in color and design creative strategies have difficulties in dealing with the fine print. The folks who create extremely detailed processes have problems seeing how those processes affect an organization's employees, customers, and investors.

To close this gap, I ensure that someone on my team is a detailed-oriented person.

I'm not a fan of relying 100% on psychometric tools. They ultimately measure how that person thinks in a calm, rational, test-taking environment. They don't tell you how s/he thinks under pressure. And I like to measure performance under pressure. I also believe that human beings are incredibly complex; a 'psycho test' simply won't be able to accurately characterize the whole person.

But psychometric tools are useful for general overviews. Psychologists say there are 4-16+ personality types. Famous personality surveys include DiSC, OCEAN, and Myers-Briggs

(MBTI). For ease of use, I prefer Peter Urs Bender's 'Bird Personality' tool.

The Bird Psychometric[2]

Before we describe Bender's test, I suggest you take it.

INSTRUCTION: In the following columns, tick those words (or phrases) that best describe you in a business or work situation. Once done, add the ticks from each column at the bottom.

GROUP A	GROUP B
❑ Reserved	❑ Take-charge attitude
❑ Uncommunicative	❑ Directive
❑ Cool	❑ Tends to use power
❑ Cautious	❑ Fast actions
❑ Guarded	❑ Risk-taker
❑ Seems difficult to get to know	❑ Competitive
❑ Demanding of self	❑ Aggressive
❑ Disciplined attitudes	❑ Strong opinions
❑ Formal speech	❑ Excitable
❑ Rational decision-making	❑ Takes social initiative
❑ Strict	❑ Makes statements
❑ Impersonal	❑ Loud voice
❑ Businesslike	❑ Quick pace
❑ Disciplined about time	❑ Expressive voice
❑ Uses facts	❑ Firm handshake
❑ Formal dress	❑ Clear idea of needs
❑ Measured actions	❑ Initiator
❑ **TOTAL**	❑ **TOTAL**

---

2   Peter Urs Bender, "Quiz," 1998, http://www.peterursbender.com/quiz/quiz.html (Accessed 28 June 2020).

<table>
<tr><td>

GROUP C

- ❑ Communicative
- ❑ Open
- ❑ Warm
- ❑ Approachable
- ❑ Friendly

- ❑ Fluid attitudes
- ❑ Informal speech
- ❑ Undisciplined about time

- ❑ Easy-going with self

- ❑ Impulsive

- ❑ Informal dress
- ❑ Dramatic opinions

- ❑ Uses opinions
- ❑ Permissive
- ❑ Emotional decision-making

- ❑ Seems easy to get to know

- ❑ Personal
- ❑ **TOTAL**

</td><td>

GROUP D

- ❑ Slow pace
- ❑ Flat voice
- ❑ Soft-spoken
- ❑ Helper
- ❑ Unclear about what is needed

- ❑ Moderate opinions
- ❑ Calm
- ❑ Asks questions

- ❑ Tends to avoid use of power

- ❑ Indifferent handshake

- ❑ Deliberate actions
- ❑ Let's others take social initiative

- ❑ Risk-avoider
- ❑ Quiet
- ❑ Go-along attitude

- ❑ Supportive

- ❑ Cooperative
- ❑ **TOTAL**

</td></tr>
</table>

Which column (group) has your largest number of total ticks?

That group is your primary personality type. If another group has only one or two ticks less than your largest group, then that group is your secondary personality type.

Bender breaks human personalities into four main bird types that I remember by the acronym DOPE.

Peaceful Dove (Group D): These are cooperative team players. They focus on group harmony. They are friendly and helpful and will experience stress when there is conflict and disharmony. There are many doves in organizations as they get along well with others. They can be found in the Customer Service, Administration, and HR departments.

Analytical Owl (Group A): These are the detailed-oriented, smart, thoughtful, and quiet folks. They keep to themselves. They may not speak up in meetings, but supervisors need to involve them as they often have well-developed ideas. They experience stress when rules aren't followed, when systems crash, when chaos happens. Owls can be found in the IT, accounting, and engineering departments.

Sociable Peacock (Group C): These are expressive, showy, creative, and talkative individuals. They require public recognition. Their ideas may not be as thought-out as an owl's, but their ideas can be more strategic and 'big picture.' They experience stress when people follow processes that don't make sense. Peacocks can be found in sales, customer service, and HR.

Decisive Eagle (Group B): These are results-oriented individuals. They like authority, power, and status. They may display their power with expensive branded items. They have a high need to achieve targets and to be in control. A lot of their self-worth is tied to their workplace status and position. They proudly display their certificates, awards, and trophies. They are stressed when it takes too long to achieve results, when deserved recognition isn't given, when losing out on a promotion, and when instructions aren't followed. Eagles can be found in senior management.

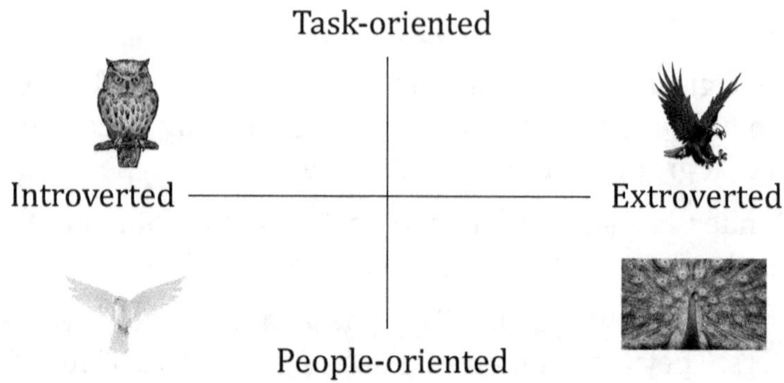

A Warning to People Who Are Both Eagle-Owls

Congratulations. You are task-oriented and driven. You are also highly detailed. You could tend to micromanage. It's important to achieve your results, but remember that you are dealing with humans, not machines. Your intentions are good because you want to improve the organization —and probably quickly. However, others can view you as a 'bull in a china shop.' Your direct impact is two-fold. Your impact on the organization is good since you can achieve and surpass targets, but if you do this in a way that negatively impacts others, your overall organizational effectiveness will decrease. People will start to complain about your working style and some of their complaints will be justified.

A Warning to People Who Are Both Peacock-Doves

Congratulations. You are people-oriented and possess a high EQ. Your teams probably like you. You could also be too soft. Fun and pleasant work environments are great, but we must still achieve results. You can be nice, but you have to hold your people accountable. Business is business.

Dealing With Different 'Birds' Post-COVID

No tool is 100% perfect (even if you use a combination of tools). But I like DOPE for a quick glance into someone's personality. If you administer it, you may want to have each employee put a picture of his or her dominant bird(s) near their workstation. It acts as a visual clue on how to talk with them. It can be fun, while reducing potential interpersonal conflicts.

In a post-COVID context, your people-focused 'Doves' and 'Peacocks' will probably feel stressed during these fast-changing times. They may require more contact from you.

Your task-focused 'Eagles' may enjoy their new-found independence, but they may get upset if their recognition and power decreases. Your 'Owls' may enjoy working remotely but get upset with process changes.

An Owl's Post-COVID Story: "How COVID Saved My Job" 

My childhood friend, Luke, is an IT programmer. He's worked with a local city government in the U.S. for 20 years. He's an older employee. Before COVID-19, he worked in an office with mostly young and middle-aged people. His new middle-aged boss gave him his first poor performance appraisal ever. The boss would frequently ask Luke, "Why aren't you retired?"

Luke felt ageism was at play and he became stressed. It affected his health which then negatively affected his work performance.

Then came COVID.

Now, Luke works from home and uploads his computer coding work back to the office. As always, his coding is excellent. His computer programs solve the city's problems. By working remotely, he's not seen as "that old, bald guy working in the corner office." He's now judged on the quality of his great output. COVID-19 saved his job and mental state. His health has also improved.

Supervising People With Diverse Personalities and Ethnicities

You will supervise people of different races, religions, genders, and marital statuses. Your job isn't easy because there is NO WAY you can keep so many different kinds of people happy. If your own personality is a dove or peacock, you are probably sensitive, friendly, and you want to be liked. That's completely natural and you shouldn't be ashamed of it.

But not everyone likes supervisors.

In my training seminars, after a particularly well-received event, many learners will say how great the training was. In the course evaluations, however, there will ALWAYS be at least one person who hated it. That's life. Don't take it personally.

Your workmates are not your housemates. They are not 'family' no matter how often disingenuous companies and senior leaders say, "Our company is a family." It's not. I'll die for my wife and my son. But don't ask me to die for one of my poor performers. If companies considered their employees to be family members, then they would contribute to the college fees that their employees pay for their children. They'd be visiting them when they are sick. They would lend or give them money for a down payment on their new house or car. Hell, the bosses would even help their employees move into their new houses. There would be no job retrenchments.

Workmates are not family members. They're workmates. As such, we all need to work hard together and produce something that can be sold to a customer. Ideally the work is conducted in a fun, safe, fair, and creative environment.

As a boss, it's impossible to cater to the various groups, cliques and informal alliances within a department. I won't even try. Instead, I will be my polite, authentic self. I have lived in over forty countries and the one commonality in every country I have visited is that people value politeness and authenticity. It applies to work, too. When people problems arise at work you may not always know what to do. But if you treat the affected people politely and authentically, you should be OK.

Surround yourself with as diverse a team as possible: this applies to genders, nationalities, races, ages, and ethnicities. The post-COVID world is a complex place and no single group has all the answers. A diverse group allows you to see issues from different perspectives and to design better solutions for diverse problems. Sure, the solutions may take longer but they will last longer. Diversity pays in the U.S. as immigrants make up 18% of America's workforce; yet they contribute 28% of the nation's high-quality patents.[3]

Management writers make a big deal about working in multi-ethnic environments. They act as if you need to be fluent in ten different languages in order to succeed. You don't. I work with Malays, Indians, Chinese, and tribal people speaking multiple languages and dialects. They pray to a multitude of gods, spirits, and ancestors while taking different religious holidays. Yet, we exceed management's targets while having fun.

I don't treat a Malay like a Malay, an Indian like an Indian, or a Mexican like a Mexican. The key is treating each person like a human. Of course, it helps to know about another's culture's nuances and particularities. It shows you took the extra effort to learn. It shows respect and care.

The same holds true with any team, multi-ethnic or not. Spend time to learn a little about each team member. You don't have to be best friends; you just need to learn a little.

I read that Alexander the Great knew the names and one fact of each of his 10,000 soldiers. I believe it. How else could you get 10,000 Greeks and Macedonians to follow (and die for you) on foot for over ten years while travelling from Greece to India? And back!

Alexander: "Hey Antigonus, how are you today?"
Antigonus: "Good your highness."
Alexander: "And does your son Demetrius still have that
          beautiful horse, Pegasus?"
Antigonus: "Yes, your highness."

---

3   Jay Shambaugh, Ryan Nunn, and Becca Portman, *Eleven Facts about Innovation and Patents,* The Hamilton Project, Brookings, December 2017, https://www.brookings.edu/wp-content/uploads/2017/12/thp_20171213_eleven_facts_innovation_patents.pdf, p. 7 (Accessed January 4, 2021).

Alexander: "Great. Give him my regards. Now be ready for today's attack. The Persians have a new chariot technology with spikes coming out from the wheel."

Antigonus: "Yes, your highness." (Antigonus, re-energized, prepares to fight like hell).

My Chapter's Key Points:

- It's good to understand your personality, but keep in mind that you are an unfinished work of art. You will never truly understand everything about yourself. That's the beauty of life.

- The Bird (DOPE) psychometric tool helps you get a rough view of your team's personality types.

- Although you will encounter people with different personalities and values from yours, you don't need to change yourself completely to treat them politely and authentically.

- Not everyone will like you (and that's OK), but everyone should understand you. And you achieve that by sharing your team's or department's values: the operating system (O/S).

You should understand each team member better than the average supervisor does. You don't need to be best friends, but a little understanding indicates a degree of care. It also helps you influence them to achieve the target. Just remember, you will never be their family member and they will never be yours.

The next chapter will help you build the right O/S to succeed.

CHAPTER 3

BUILDING THE RIGHT SYSTEMS AND PROCESSES (O/S)

*If you quit on the process, you are
quitting on the result.*
– Idowa Koyenikan, author and organizational consultant

COVID has changed economies, jobs, and business models.[4] The Prime Minister of Australia warned that his country needs to prepare for a post-COVID world that is "poorer, more dangerous, and more disorderly." Extrapolating from World Bank numbers, *The Economist* estimates that COVID cost the world USD 10.3 trillion from 2020-2021.[5]

COVID has affected you, me, your company, and your teams. For years, pre-COVID, employees have been asking for flexi-hours and work-from-home work schedules from their HR departments. And HR would reply with, "We can't monitor you." Or "Maybe one of these days" and "Management won't allow it." Then, with the advent of COVID, flexi-hours and re-mote-based jobs suddenly became doable throughout the

4　　　Quoted in Jade Macmillan and Andrew Greene, "Australia to Spend $270b Building Larger Military to Prepare for 'Poorer More Dangerous' World and Rise of China," *Australian Broadcasting Corporation*, June 30, 2020, www.abc.net.au/news/2020-06-30/australia-unveils-10-year-defence-strategy/12408232 (Accessed 1 July 2020).
5　　　"What is the Economic Cost of COVID-19?" *The Economist,* January 9, 2021, https://www.economist.com/finance-and-economics/2021/01/09/what-is-the-economic-cost-of-covid-19?frsc=dg%7Ce (Accessed January 10, 2021).

world — virtually overnight. Did you even know what WFH meant before COVID?

COVID will affect most (if not all) of the systems and processes your team use. How you design and tweak your systems and processes will determine your and your team's success.

As a young man, I worked as a temporary bill collector for Egghead Discount Software in Washington state. Egghead was the world's largest software retailer at the time. It had hundreds of brick-and-mortar stores throughout the U.S. I was responsible for collecting the Los Angeles corporate accounts. Most of the companies I collected were in the entertainment, aircraft, defense, and IT sectors. The >90-day overdue receivable level was 19%. Egghead was great at selling, but horrible at collecting. After three months, I reduced the level to 11%. They offered me a permanent job. I declined.

I saw that no matter how hard I worked; I wouldn't be able to reduce the delinquency rate to low single digits. This was due to their poor debt collection system, an incorrect billing system, and a poor sales tracking system that attached little accountability to the salespeople to ensure that their customers paid up. To me, it seemed like the company was giving away their products, not selling them.

All Egghead stores eventually closed down after the Internet arrived. The company slowly went bankrupt.

I took another temp job as a bill collector at a new wireless phone company. Their IT systems were top notch. Their billing was 99% correct. The bad debt rates were below 2% of sales. They had monthly employee performance incentive schemes. The place was well-organized. They offered me a permanent job and I took it. The company is now part of America's largest wireless phone service provider: Verizon Wireless.

Dear readers, this chapter may be the book's most important. It discusses why and how you need to the right foundation (aka 'operating system') for your team to succeed. The chapter's flow is as follows:

1. Setting the right O/S with the right values

2. Interviewing and hiring the right people to achieve the desired results

3. Onboarding your people so that they understand the O/S

4. Training your people

5. Using an additional performance model to help you achieve your results

Results = Processes X Resources

Your results are dependent on your processes multiplied by your resources. Your resources are your people, equipment, IT systems, budget, time, energy, political capital, organizational network, information, and yourself. And, year after year, organizations push us to increase results while reducing our resources. This principle is known as "Do More with Less." It causes stress and anxiety (but then that's life).

If your organization regularly reduces your resources — while expecting the same or better results — then your best chance of succeeding is by improving your team's processes. You may be resource poor, but that doesn't mean you can't be resourceful.

In Malaysia, I ran an 80-person debt collection contact center at a wireless phone service provider. In any job with many employees and a million customers, there are many movable parts and systems. Every now and then, processes or resources will be compromised — which then impacts your monthly results.

The best people to help you improve work processes are often at hand. Your team members are experts on how these processes help or hinder their results. Since you have emphasized the value of creativity and courage, they will hopefully share their process-improvement ideas with you.

But this is hard for many bosses because they fear losing control. Instead of the team showing the boss how to improve their results, the boss wants to tell them how to improve. They ignore the team's collective wisdom. As Samuel Culbert argues in the *Wall Street Journal*:

> the most important relationship in any organization—between a boss and an employee—is too often a farce. It isn't, 'How can we work together to get results?' It's, 'How can I, the boss, force you to become more like me, even if we all suffer because of it?'[6]

Besides learning from your team's wisdom, also turn to your peers for additional ideas.

Finally, your immediate superior has a wealth of ideas. My good past bosses didn't see our problems with the level of detail that my team and I did. Yet, they could view it from a higher perspective and share their unique insights.

When you involve others in the process, you get increased buy-in (especially from your boss) and better solutions. This smoothens the path to enact the change.

On my first day working with Andrew Gan, my former boss (and friend), "Steve", he said, "the department runs pretty smoothly. We've finally got all the processes, systems, and people running well. I just need your help to ensure things don't break."

He was right.

---

6   Samuel A. Culbert, "How the Pandemic Can Turn Bad Bosses into Good Ones", *Wall Street Journal*, August 2, 2020. https://www.wsj.com/articles/how-the-pandemic-can-turn-bad-bosses-into-good-ones-11596210436 (Accessed August 30, 2020).

The processes were highly automated, thus reducing the chances of human error. Every Sunday and Wednesday night, the billing system would automatically bar 10,000 customers' cell phone lines (for non-payment or for exceeding their credit limit). On Monday and Thursday mornings, my team would be hit by thousands of angry customers. Their phone lines had been hot-lined into our collection department. Once they paid their bills, the system would automatically reinstate their service within thirty minutes. Our department of 80 people serviced one million lines.

You can win with the right processes. Some people call them 'strategies' — you can succeed with them even if you don't have the best resources. There are many examples of this happening in the corporate world. Many believe Apple's operating system is better than Microsoft's. But why are the vast majority of PCs running Windows? Microsoft's process (strategy) was to price it lower than Apple's and allow more PC manufacturers to install it. Why does Coke outsell Pepsi when most taste-tests surveys show that people prefer the sweeter Pepsi? Why does McDonald's sell so many hamburgers when most people consider its food to be barely palatable? It's probably because of their strategy of using children's playgrounds and toys in their restaurants, plus great fries.

A recent example of organizations running with excellent processes and the right level of resources to achieve fantastic results are the world's drug companies' in creating COVID vaccines. Drugs that used to take years (or decades) to develop were rolled out in less than a year — from 11 March 2020 (when the WHO declared a pandemic) to 11 December 2020 (when Pfizer got U.S. FDA approval).

The equation: Results = Processes X Resources also applies to countries. I've lived and travelled in over 40 countries. Some have better designed laws (systems and processes) than others. Some countries are more prosperous, cleaner, safer, and less corrupt than others. Why? Is it because one nation's people are innately more honest while another's is more corrupt?

I don't think so.

It has to do with the systems and processes and how nations use their resources. Singapore is one of the least corrupt and richest nations on the planet. Yet, it is based in a region with some of the most corrupt countries on the planet. Why?

In Singapore, you get fined for jaywalking. In the rest of Southeast Asia, jaywalking is a national sport. In Singapore, offering a bribe to a public servant will land you in jail. In the rest of Southeast Asia, you may get a 'thank you.' People operate according to the operating system they live and work in.

If your team's or department's processes and systems are logical, fair, and supported; you will have a good chance to succeed. If your processes and systems are unfair, haphazard, and disliked; your people will conduct themselves in the appropriate manner to succeed in that environment and you will probably fail.

I dislike supervisors who blame their teams for their poor results. I understand if 10-15% of a team consists of poor performers, but it's rare that 100% are underperforming. It's not always the team that has the problem. It's either the systems and processes, or the supervisor.

If you play by the rules of volleyball, you play a game called "volleyball." If you play by the rules of basketball, you play a game called "basketball." If your work team plays by nasty, unfair, or confusing rules; then they are playing a nasty and brutish game. Setting the right processes and systems (your O/S) will create the right environment for your team to succeed.

Values

Your company has its own values; you need to inculcate those values in your teams. The problem with corporate values is that they mostly sound the same. Or there are so many values that employees forget them. Or the company never emphasizes the values after the employee's first day on the job.

Besides corporate values, add some team or department values. It shows your team how you think. The values can come from them, but a few must come from you. As an employee, how many times have you felt that you couldn't understand how your boss thinks? Setting team values is one way to show your team your O/S. Your team—whether your organization knows it or not—follows your O/S.

In my O/S, I value courage and ethics. And I want my people to display those two values. In addition, I value a performance-based work system, not a prejudiced-based one. I want everyone to know that we succeed or fail based on each person's performance. I've been accused of having favorites. And I agree. I tell them, "You can be my favorite too if you perform like her." As Deng Xiaoping famously said, "I don't care if the cat is black or white as long as it catches mice."

Post-COVID, some of your team's values may change. For example, flexibility and continuous learning may become more important than before. Your team will also have written and unwritten values. If you have remote-based employees, you may want to write down the previously unwritten values to reduce future miscommunication. It's easy to forget – or not know – the unwritten team values when you work remotely.

Tsedal Neely, a Harvard Business School professor, offers a vision of the future in *Remote Work Revolution* (2021):

> ... most remote teams would benefit from a charter or 'prenup'—a document that group members write together to spell out expectations and boundaries. One way to develop such a prenup for an existing group is to have a facilitator first ask people to list the key (if unspoken) team norms. Next, people discuss which 'shalts' and 'shall nots' ought to be kept, subtracted and added.

Then they select and commit to six or seven core agreements (long lists are hard to remember and become oppressive).

For example, many companies are adopting a norm for shorter meetings. After I spoke about prenups, an engineer in my class convinced her newly virtual team to write one. They decided their old one-hour meeting norm was fueling Zoom fatigue, so they changed it to 45 minutes.[7]

Creativity and fun are two other key values for me. I want each team member to use their creative-thinking muscles. I don't want them switching off their brains at work. If they see that the job can be improved, they need to alert me. If they find problems, they need to alert me. As automation becomes more and more entrenched at work, creativity may be the #1 most important trait that you can develop in your people to prepare them for an uncertain future.

Fun. I want people to enjoy the work, each other, the company, and the customers. If they don't enjoy me, the boss, that's OK. But I still want them to enjoy the rest.

By having the right mix of values, you will have a better chance of having a top performing, motivated team. But nothing is guaranteed.

Here is a list of values. Choose a few to incorporate in your team's O/S:

• Business-savviness	• Integrity	• Respectful
• Customer-focused	• Profit-minded	• Innovative
• Fairness	• Fun	• Flexibility

---

7   Robert I. Sutton, "Remote Work Is Here to Stay. Bosses Better Adjust," *Wall Street Journal*, August 2, 2020, https://www.wsj.com/articles/remote-work-is-here-to-stay-bosses-better-adjust-11596395367 (Accessed August 30, 2020).

• Continuous Improvement	• Results-focused	• Open communication
• Continuous Learning	• Honesty	• Excellence
• Creative / Critical thinking	• Change-orientated	• Cultural diversity
• Teamwork	• Helpful	• Safe
• Performance-based	• Model the values	• Purposeful
• Kindness	• Quality	• Quantity

It's Not About Culture

Management consultants talk a lot about the importance of creating the right corporate culture. They make it sound as if culture is everything. I agree that culture is important. Culture is based upon the rules of that group of employees.

And those rules (systems and processes) are repeated over and over until they become part of individuals' and groups' operating systems. Aren't they really just habits? When I hear CEOs and management consultants talking about 'culture-building initiatives', my eyes glaze over. Aren't these initiatives just about putting in place the right systems and processes to help an organization or team to excel?

I like walking into a Starbucks. And it's not just because they come from my hometown, Seattle. I like their operating system (O/S). Their O/S includes welcoming you with a smile and calling your first name when your drink is ready. Their staff are hired according to their ability to believe and follow their O/S. Starbucks has put in place the right values, systems, and processes to charge you more than other coffee shops. And you pay it.

Isn't your primary role as a supervisor, boss, or leader (or whatever you call yourself) to build the right environment where each team member is able to perform at his or her best? In essence, you're building a community of people who follow a set of positive values and behaviors. If done well, your people will feel strongly attached to their community.

Don't Just Focus on Your Team

Your team is dependent on other teams to achieve success. These other teams can be within your own department or outside. In my case, my Collections department was dependent on the Credit department as they determined the number of credit limit barrings. The IT department was important as we were highly automated and needed their systems to be operational — otherwise the system would crash. The Finance department was needed to provide aging reports, track performance, and set monthly collection targets (and pay us a monthly incentive if we hit our targets). The Customer Service department was important as many of our customers visited branches to make payments. The Payment Processing department ensured that payments from multiple payment channels were applied correctly and promptly.

You need to forge deep peer and superior contacts in departments that are critical to your team's success. If I could go back in time, I would have spent more time cultivating peer and superior relationships in those key departments that affected my department the most, and less time on my teams. I could have then used my in-depth peer and superior contacts to resolve more of my teams' problems faster, achieved better results, and increased their confidence in me.

With strong relationships throughout the company, your influence will increase. Your team will see you as someone with 'jalan' (a Malay word that literally means 'road', but also used colloquially to refer to the power to get things done). Your organizational network will also help you get promotions, transfers, and even jobs in other organizations. Raising your organizational visibility is not wrong. Many of your current organizational contacts will leave for better jobs at other companies (even companies that compete with yours). If they have a good opinion of you, they can refer you to them one day. At one Malaysian employer, our CEO left to join a competitor. He then offered many of us at his old employer great new job opportunities at his new employer—if you knew him.

You don't achieve your best results by working hard day after day while focusing all of your time on your team. Networking helps both you and your team. As they say in Malaysia, "Get out from under the coconut shell."

Supervising with Fairness

We've discussed how you can promote various team values: creativity, courage, ethics, performance-based, and fun. Now, I'd like to dwell on another: fairness. If I had to give you only one bit of advice to be a better supervisor or leader, it would be this: **be fair.**

How did you feel as a young child when your dad gave candy to your brother and not you? What did you say to him? "Dad, that's not..."

Humans want life to be fair. We have legal codes and regulations to ensure that society is fair. Otherwise, we protest. Of course, life isn't fair — but we still try to make it as fair as possible.

Even animals understand fairness. Try rewarding two dogs differently. After a while, the one who isn't rewarded will start to ignore your commands. A doggie protest.

Not all your team members will like you: that's life. Who likes supervisors? There is even an app called *Beat the Boss* by Game Hive Corporation. It has 20 million downloads and is on its fourth version. People are envious that you make more money and have more power than them. But, if I asked the team members who dislike you if you are a fair boss, they would (hopefully) say, "Yes."

I'd much prefer being disliked and considered fair than being liked and considered unfair. I doubt anyone would truly like an unfair boss. Fair bosses are consistent. They apply the same rules for everyone, even for themselves.

When new parents, overwhelmed with the job of raising nice children, ask for my advice, I keep it simple: tell your children that you love them and are proud of them. That's it. Your children will forgive your many parenting mistakes when they become adults because they will realize you meant well. When I see supervisors overwhelmed with people-management issues, I advise them to be fair.

Getting the Right People on the Bus

Jim Collins, author of *Good to Great* (2001), writes about the importance of attracting and keeping the right people on the bus — in the right seats.[8] And the importance of getting the wrong people off the bus. Ideally, I'd go even further and prevent certain people from boarding the bus in the first place.

One of my heroes (possibly because my home state is named after him) is George Washington: America's first president. Although he wasn't the smartest soldier in the American Revolutionary army, Washington had excellent skills in hiring and promoting talent. He found the right people and put them in the right seats on his bus. Performance was at the top of his criteria and it overruled age or nationality. (But it didn't override race or gender at that time).

He modelled the leadership requirements of courage and ethics to get his team to turn his rag-tag army into a respectable fighting force that defeated the world's superpower at that time.

His diverse 'bus riders' were from all over the world and from all age groups. Places like the Caribbean, France, the U.K., Prussia, and Poland. His bus had young people like Mar-

---

8   Jim Collins, Good to Great: *Why Some Companies Make the Leap ...and Others Don't* (New York: HarperCollins, 2001), 13.

quis de Lafayette (aged 19), Nathanael Greene (33), Alexander Hamilton (20), Henry Knox (25), Anthony Wayne (30), Thaddeus Kosciuszko (29), Benjamin Tallmadge (21), and John Laurens (21).[9]

He didn't practice ageism. Seated with the youngsters were older gents like Francis Marion (43), William Moultrie (45), and Fredrich Wilhelm Baron von Steuben (45). The average life expectancy during this era was 36.

Washington also had a slave on his bus: William (Billy) Lee. He was Washington's valued valet. Lee was at his side in all battles and hardships, including during the bitter winter at Valley Forge. He was freed upon Washington's death.[10]

Together, these bus riders added skills that Washington lacked such as military engineering, training, proficiency in French, spy craft, knowledge of local geography, and military strategy. His supervisory style kept these top performers united and motivated in supporting the common goal: independence.

He must have been a good boss as his team supported him at crucial moments in his career. During the early stages of the war, when seditious unsigned documents circulated — supporting General Horatio Gates' ambitions to replace Washington--it was his 'bus riders' who stood up to defeat this threat that allowed Washington to continue as Commander-in-Chief and eventual victory.

Their support for him also saved the U.S. from becoming a military dictatorship. After the U.S. achieved its indepen-

---

9   "Washington's Officers and Gentlemen," *George Washington's Mount Vernon,* https://www.mountvernon.org/george-washington/the-revolutionary-war/washingtons-officers/ (Accessed August 1, 2020).

10   Washington is one of the U.S.'s few founding fathers who freed his slaves. In his last will and testament, it stipulated that upon his wife's (Martha's) death, all 123 of his slaves were to be freed. And she freed them even sooner: just one year after George's death. Incidentally, Martha had her own slaves and all 153 of them were *not* freed upon her death. See Erin Blakemore, "Did George Washington Really Free Mount Vernon Enslaved Workers?", October 11, 2017, *History.com,* https://www.history.com/news/did-george-washington-really-free-mount-vernons-slaves (Accessed November 18, 2020).

dence, General Gates wanted to overthrow the new government to demand unpaid wages. Washington objected, arguing that democracy was preferable to a chaotic, military-style junta (probably helmed by Gates). Gates and Washington gave their opposing speeches for and against the military coup that is now known as the Newburgh Conspiracy. With his dream team supporting him, Washington — and democracy — won the day.

Choose Your People Wisely

Many supervisors hire quickly. They reckon the quicker they can get the new resource working, the quicker s/he can improve the team's results. But, like choosing a spouse, snap hiring judgments will sink you. You will not achieve operational and career success if you have a lousy team.

Some supervisors delegate the interviewing and hiring decision to their subordinates. I don't. My department's success is directly impacted by the quality of my people. So, I'm involved in designing the job requirements, the interview questions, conducting the interviews, negotiating with HR on other details, and the final selection process. I will likely spend more waking hours with that person than with my own family, so I want to reduce the chances of making a hiring mistake.

When I interview people, I'm looking for many things. I'm looking for strengths that I have identified as critical for the job in question. I'm also looking for strengths that my team lacks. I'm also looking to catch a glimpse of that candidate's attitude and values.

This next section focuses on the areas of interviewing, onboarding, and training new staff to become great performers.

Interviewing

I'm actively involved in interviewing applicants. It's the best way to judge another human being (albeit in a relatively superficial manner). It works much better than looking at resumes, evaluating psychometric surveys, and viewing LinkedIn profiles. I try to conduct the interview in a minimum of 1.5 hours, if not longer. I want to interview the employee for any team in my department, even if s/he won't report directly to me. If I like him or her, then I'll recommend the applicant for an interview with their future supervisor. I try to keep the interview conversational and relaxed as I can discover more information from the applicant.

Job applicants have practiced their 'interview spiel' for years. They can come across as polished during the interview. Once hired, however, they can be lousy employees. And vice versa. I like taking at least 1.5 hours as I find that most people can't maintain their 'interview spiel' longer than an hour. They start to make mistakes and run out of prepared stories.

Interview Questions

I've discovered it's much easier to correct a team member's skill and knowledge shortcomings than one's attitude and values. I prefer interview questions that allow me to glimpse into the applicant's internal operating system (O/S).

Such questions cover:

- Who is s/he really?
- What motivates him or her?
- What kind of people, organization, and boss do they like and dislike?
- What does s/he value?
- What does s/he fear?
- What's his or her ideal work environment?
- What parts of the current job does s/he like the best and least?
- What causes him or her stress?
- What's him or her ideal job?

- How does s/he problem solve?
- Why did s/he decide on this career?
- Why did s/he leave their last job?
- What are some crucial decisions s/he had to make in life?

Hopefully, by understanding a bit of the job applicant's O/S, you will see if that person fits into your team's systems, processes, and culture. If s/he is hired, you and your team will spend hours with that person. There is nothing worse than being around someone who doesn't share the same values as you and your team. Don't put yourselves through hell by making a hiring mistake. You better be damn sure about that person before hiring.

Of course, if you are hiring people for technical positions, you need them to give you the correct calculations, programing code, drawings, and answers to see if they have the technical skills to do that job. But not all jobs have black and white criteria for success.

Technical jobs require a lot of knowledge, but non-technical jobs require less knowledge as the new hire will likely be schooled in the new company's unique knowledge once s/he joins. In fact, their previous work knowledge might not transfer 100%. Knowledge is secondary.

Technical jobs also require applicants to display the right kind of attitudes and interpersonal skills. Unfortunately, employers focus too much on the technical skills and knowledge requirements of the post. They overlook the attitudes and interpersonal skills that are required to succeed in that post. People get hired for their technical skills, but I find that most people get fired (or promoted) for non-technical reasons.

Normally, I will choose an applicant with a great attitude and interpersonal skills, even if they only have a so-so knowledge level — versus another applicant with a so-so attitude and great knowledge. Team members with poor attitudes and interpersonal skills cause havoc and discord. They will take up your time. It's easier to train team members with knowledge gaps vs. attitudinal and interpersonal skill gaps.

As a kid, I asked my dad, an ophthalmologist, how long it would take for me to learn his job. I thought he'd say something like, "Never." Instead, he said, "If you observed me every day, after two years you could probably do about 90% of it." He said the remaining 10% would be the rare eye cases that I wouldn't know anything about. He said being a doctor is like being a mechanic, except you work on the human body. Anybody with a reasonable brain can pick it up.

Hypothetical Interview Questions

Most interviewers dislike hypothetical questions. They consider them unfair and stupid, but I like them. I just don't ask too many. I like to give candidates tough hypothetical situations to see how they think on their feet. For non-technical jobs, I'm unconcerned if their final output is correct or incorrect. I just want to see if they have the courage to try and the power to create. The worst an applicant could say is, "I don't know." Or, "I would ask my boss." To me, courage and creativity can't be taught to adults. They should already display these attributes.

For example, if I was hiring a customer-facing employee, I would ask, "What would you say if a customer said…?"

Interview Assignment Tasks

When I was hiring for a corporate trainer position, I said: "In the next 15 minutes, please design a 1-day course titled "Selling Product X." I'll need your course goal, objectives, and key modules." If an applicant couldn't do such a basic assignment, I would conclude the interview.

In one organization, I was hiring for an internal technical training position right before a major retrenchment exercise. I could save someone's job. Three applicants from the retrenchment list applied. I asked each to email me a list of technical courses that s/he can conduct. Of the three, only one completed this simple task. I gave the job to him. The other two were retrenched. As a hiring manager, if someone can't complete a simple task to save their own job, how will s/he perform on other tasks?

Competency-based Questions

These questions are popular, useful, and realistic since you are asking about the person's past work experience. They usually start with the words, "Tell me about a time where you..." This is a good interviewing technique. You should ask some of these questions but be aware that the candidates have rehearsed their responses many, many times. They're expecting these questions.

Examples:

- "Tell me a time where you missed a deadline."
- "Tell me a time where you had to work with a difficult boss."
- "Tell me a time where you had to work with a team."
- "Tell me about the rudest customer you dealt with this year."

Based on their responses, you can then drill down for more details. You could even fact-check them later. It's usually in the drilling down that you learn more about the candidate.

Examples:

- "And why did that happen?"
- "What did you learn from that?"
- "How did it make you feel?"
- "What could have been improved?"
- "Why did you say 'nothing'? Are you saying it was perfect?"

Interview Story for a Training Manager's Post (Asking Oddball Questions)

My employer had an open training manager position and I needed to interview a couple applicants. One question that I use frequently to gain a glimpse into someone's O/S is, "If you were to receive a surprise $5,000 (RM20,000) today. What would you spend it on?"

Most people don't expect such oddball questions. One applicant said, "Clothes." Another said, "Training books." It wasn't a make-or-break question for me, but it did leave me wondering if such a person would fit into my team. Would the team like a boss who thought a lot about clothes? Would the team like a boss who was probably lying and said, "Training books"?

Besides my team, could I even work with such people?

Fact Checking

Although interviewing is a critical piece of the hiring puzzle, you also need to fact check their statements and accomplishments. This is more important, but rarely done. The best predictor of future behavior is past behavior. Too often we neglect their past and only look at their 'blue sky' speeches of how they will help our team succeed in the future. If any of my past top performers listed me as a reference, I would gladly share my experience with them to any future employer.

My first impressions on applicants are often wrong. It's better to evaluate that applicant by fact checking with his or her past employers. They have spent years with that person. If the job you have open is similar with their last job, you need to determine if their past employers consider him or her a top, average, or poor performer. It's rare that a poor employee — while working in a similar job — suddenly becomes a top performer.

What will happen if you hire someone without fact checking? HR will eventually discover that the person lied about his or her past accomplishments, skills, knowledge, qualifications, and education. You can guess who will get the blame.

> **✍Tip:**
>
> If you hire a great person, the organization will give you little recognition for your wise decision. But, if you hire a horrible person, you will certainly get lots of bad recognition: "Hey, who hired that jerk?" This is especially painful when it comes from your own team.

Onboarding Process

The applicant has successfully passed the interviews with multiple people and departments. The background check was positive and now s/he is hired.

Now what?

It's time to put him or her through an onboarding process. HR people will tell you that onboarding is about socializing new people vs. orientating them. It sounds good, but all I want to do is to shape the new team member to the new work environment. You will not get another opportunity to shape a team member at such a formative stage.

Onboarding is a process, not a one-off event. One of my past employers had a 90-day onboarding process where new employees had to visit various departments to see the organization's big picture. And ALL new employees spent one week doing a customer-facing job to understand the value of customers.

You want your new hire to understand:

- What are the rules (systems, processes, and values) that your team and employer operate by?

- Why senior people support these rules? I suggest you invite a senior leader to meet the new hires.

- How to succeed in the work environment? What does success look like here? Invite a top performer to talk about this topic to give it more credibility. They will believe him/her more than you.

- What is expected of them? And why they are critical to the team's success?

- Who's who in the team and department? Building good relationships is vital for success.

- Who are our key internal and external customers that we must please?

Hopefully, the new hire learnt the rules during the interview process. Now s/he can SEE the rules in action. Ideally, the new hire has already adopted the rules. If your team's O/S compliments the new hire's O/S, then you will have a better chance of retaining that staff. Hopefully your team's O/S attracts good applicants. Of course, a good O/S needs to be supported by competitive salaries, benefits packages, and developmental opportunities.

Post-COVID, onboarding new team members will be difficult if most of their fellow team members (and even the boss) are working remotely. How do you maintain their new job excitement? How do they understand the written and unwritten rules of working there? How do they become friendly with their new team members?

One idea is to pair the new team member with an experienced team member (buddy system) who acts as a guide to navigate the organization. S/he introduces the new team member to the other team members, key organizational contacts, and teaches him or her about the organization's technology platforms to maintain communication.

Training Process

I've spent half my career in the education and training fields. I've found that the best kind of training is on-the-job-training. Increasing a team member's responsibilities with on-the-job assignments are a great learning tool, especially when they fail. Failure causes pain and pain is a great teacher. Of course, you just don't want them failing on critical projects, so use your discretion on the assignments that you feel they can handle. When they succeed, it builds confidence: *"Competence breeds confidence."* On particularly difficult projects, you will need to check-in with them to ensure that they stay on track and increase their chances for success.

I like awarding special projects to my top performers as developmental opportunities. The top performers, my 'Stars', can get away from their normal work routines and try something new. Special projects allow them to learn practical skills and gain responsibilities than they would never have received in a formal, external training event.

My friend Linda Teh worked at an oil company. Although she was an HR manager that specialized in staffing, her organization required its employees to rotate to a different department every two to three years. I thought this was a fantastic system. Let's face it, our work futures are becoming more and more uncertain. There will be jobs in the next ten years that we have never heard of today. Other jobs will die. What better way to future-proof your employees than by helping them develop new skills?

Still, formal training events do have benefits:

- They give employees the confidence to try something new back on-the-job. Some supervisors lack time to frequently coach their team members, so external training helps. When learners come to my training, sometimes years after they were hired for the position, many say that I have helped relieve their stress after learning new skills and knowledge. Before the training, they were just doing their job as best as they knew how.

- Training events give people a break from their jobs. It allows them to think vs. react. These events allow people to fine-tune their skills and increase their knowledge while having fun. It also improves teamwork.

- They act as a reward. When you send a team member to external training, you are showing that you care enough about that person to allow him or her to leave the workplace, develop themselves, and have fun. It helps retain staff.

- They help employees get new ideas and techniques from external trainers. We spend our careers with people inside the same department and employer. We understand how things are done in our own environment, but not always how it's done outside. Your people can also network and learn from others in the same field.

Besides formal training events, conferences and conventions accomplish many of the same results. Again, the attendees have a chance to travel and network with others in their field.

The Importance of HR, Post-COVID

Pre-COVID HR was a support team that in many organizations made a minimal impact. It was rarely felt except on pay day, promotions, and trainings. However, post-COVID the work rules have changed. What was one of the least innovative departments in organizations will need to radically redesign itself to become one of the most innovative.

HR questions that arise post-COVID, especially for remote workers

- If someone works from home while sick, is that counted as a sick day? Or half a day?

- What happens if the WFH sick person works, but can't produce 100% of the results? Do they get scolded for missing the target? Or do they get praised for trying to work while they were sick?

- Will remote workers be paid an extra stipend or allowance?

- Will the office seating environment be open or closed?

- How does the organization measure and monitor the remote workforce?

- Do team members have to work fixed hours or can they be flexi-hours to allow them to take care of their children and other personal matters?

- Who pays for their chair, desk, internet service, PC, and other materials used to do their jobs? What happens to this equipment if the team member leaves?

- What happens if a remote employee is injured while working at home? Does the employer's or the homeowner's insurance cover it?

- How are vacation leaves calculated? Can people take a half-day off? Quarter-day?

- Do you onboard new people remotely? Or do you bring them into the office for a day or two to meet key people and understand the corporate and team values?

- How do we contact team members if their home internet or phone connection goes down? Alternate contact numbers? Neighbors' numbers?

- If some of your remote team members are suddenly permanently or temporarily retrenched, is there a process to help them apply for government assistance quickly?

These are just a few. I know my HR friends are busy drafting work policies as this book is being written.

RACE Performance Model (Results, Activities, Competencies, Enablers)

Sashee Raman, DBA (my colleague) has created another model that can help your team and company achieve stellar results. It's called RACE.[11]

---

11   Sasheedran Raman, "RACE Performance Model," 2020, *Paradigm Learning Consultancy,* www.paradigmasia.com.my, +60 19 319-3999.

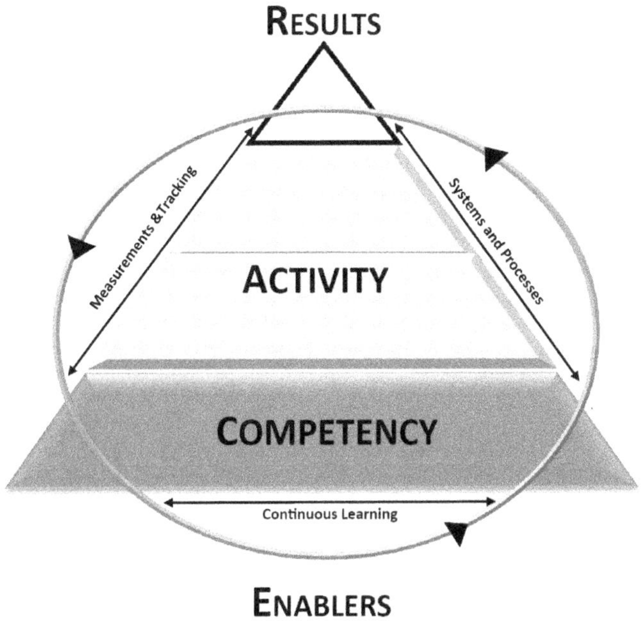

Results

Results are the goal that you and your team need to achieve. The results are set by you or by senior management. But before you can achieve the results, you first need to define the vital activities your people must do and the competencies they must have. The simpler your definitions, the easier it is for your team to understand them.

For example, at my past employer the key result was to reduce bad debt to below 2% of sales. We then defined the work activities and HR competencies needed to help us achieve that result. This narrow focus helped us eliminate time wasting activities that distracted us from that result.

Activities

These are the critical daily functions the team needs to perform to achieve the desired results. Unfortunately, a lot of our team's time is wasted on activities that don't DIRECTLY contribute to the results. These could include: attending unimportant meetings, responding to unimportant emails, putting out organizational fires, creating unimportant reports, and getting side-tracked by other teams' requests.

Only you will know the few key activities that need to be done to achieve your results. Your people's management and monitoring skills need to be honed towards prioritizing critical activities. Just like a soccer team, every player has his or her specific role to make the team win. Similarly, as a supervisor you would need to assign tasks and duties — with the right tracking mechanism — to ensure that your team performs optimally.

Competencies

These are the required attitudes, skills, and knowledge that your team needs to perform the activities. As the supervisor, you need to develop your team members — and close certain gaps — so that the team can perform the activities well. Competencies form the bedrock of the RACE model. Without a solid base, your team will fail.

Back to the soccer team analogy: each player needs help on improving his or her skills and motivation levels to ensure victory. A good coach develops each team member's skills to increase confidence and bring out the best from your players.

Enablers

These support the Results, Activities, and Competencies. Sashee views them as the engine to keep the three sections moving.

There are three kinds of enablers:

1. **Measurements and Tracking:** These are your monitoring tools to generate the reports and data that shows your achievements in the Results, Activities, and Competencies areas. They act as scorecards to tell you whether your team is winning or losing. "If it's not tracked, it

won't get done." A word of warning: avoid measuring and tracking everything. Overloading management with reports- most of which aren't read—is a waste of resources. It also can be oppressive on your team and take time away from them to complete the crucial activities.

Measuring and tracking also helps you also see bottlenecks and provide the team with the right tools to remove them such as PCs, workspace, internet connections, raw materials, additional staff, and whatever else. In the new WFH environment, bosses will take a more active back-end role to ensure their team gets what they need to do their jobs.

Post-COVID, will require different measurements — especially if you have remote team members. For example, ensuring that your team is sitting at their workstations at certain times of the day may be less important now than if they complete a certain number of activities each day. The day-to-day managing people may be less important than managing their work.

2. **Systems and Processes:** This is your team's O/S. Once in place, it ensures that the Results are achieved, the Activities are completed, and the Competencies are developed.

3. **Continuous Learning**: This applies mostly to the competency section. It ensures that your people develop the right attitudes, skills, and knowledge to perform the activities and achieve the results. Continuous learning also applies to the enablers to further improve your measurement and tracking systems, while fine-tuning your team and organizational O/S.

My Chapter's Key Points:

- Results = Processes X Resources. It's rare that you will receive lots of resources, so processes are the key to achieving your results. To maximize your resources, you need to put in place the right rules, values, processes, or systems (e.g., culture). Once in place, you have a better chance of achieving your results.

- An influential supervisor spends a large portion of his or her job networking with peers and superiors, not just with the team. A good organizational network helps you remove interdepartmental roadblocks. As a result, your team will see you as someone with influence. You will make a bigger organizational impact while increasing your value.

- Take time interviewing, onboarding, and training your team members. You can't win championships with lousy players. Senior management and your team will remember you if you hire poor performers.

- The RACE (Results-Activities-Competencies-Enablers) Performance Model helps you visualize the necessary factors that need to be put in place to achieve the desired results.

Once your team's O/S has been designed, you next need to communicate it. The next chapter shares unique and practical communication models to implement the O/S.

CHAPTER 4

COMMUNICATING WITH TEAM, PEERS, BOSS, & SENIOR MANAGEMENT

Words are, of course, the most powerful drug used by mankind.
– Rudyard Kipling, British writer

Your success is determined by how well you communicate with your team, your peers, your customers, your suppliers, your boss, senior management, investors, and the board. Neurologists claim that half of our brain capacity is devoted to the sense of sight. Your communication skills will inevitably affect how others see you. The results you achieve at work will often be less important than how others see and perceive you.

If you consider your and your team's communication skills to be top-notch, then I suggest you skim through this chapter and then move on. For most of us, however, having formal communication structures in place go a long way in reducing miscommunication. Miscommunications will cost you money, time, and relationships. We have all suffered the pain of miscommunicating. Either by little mistakes like telling another person a wrong date or time for a meeting, or bigger ones like calling a current romantic partner or spouse by an old partner's name. It happens. The key is to minimize them.

A key difference between successful and unsuccessful companies (and teams) lies in the level of miscommunication. Companies with good internal and external communication structures have a better chance at succeeding. The 19th century Prussian Field Marshall, Helmuth von Moltke, said it best: *"No plan survives first contact with the enemy."*

It's easy to see communication break downs in the sporting world. Coaches and players will start the game with a wonderful game plan, but that quickly falls apart once the opposing team counters it. Coaches call for time outs to re-strategize and communicate new plans. At the end of the game, all else being equal, the losing team is usually the one that failed to communicate their and their opponent's plans the best.

In the post-COVID era, our communication channels have increased — along with the importance of communicating well. Post-COVID, our organization's and our competitors' plans have changed. These changes need to be communicated well and often. Post-COVID — especially if you have remote team members — it's best to err on the side of over-communication.

Your personal communication skills will affect your career progression. We have all seen top performers passed over for promotion — overshadowed by a subpar but more eloquent employee. My wife calls such people 'empty vessels,' but many 'empty vessels' aren't so empty. Some have great communication (and interpersonal) skills that allow them to blame other people, departments, or events (IT system crashes, COVID-19, the economy, etc.) for their frequent failures.

When I communicate with my team, I like to use a formal communication model that my colleague, Jude Louis (www. oscarpresentationskills.com) and I developed. It's called ACCT and it helps to reduce miscommunications within the team. It is particularly useful for sharing instructions and strategies.

The ACCT Model for Communicating Instructions

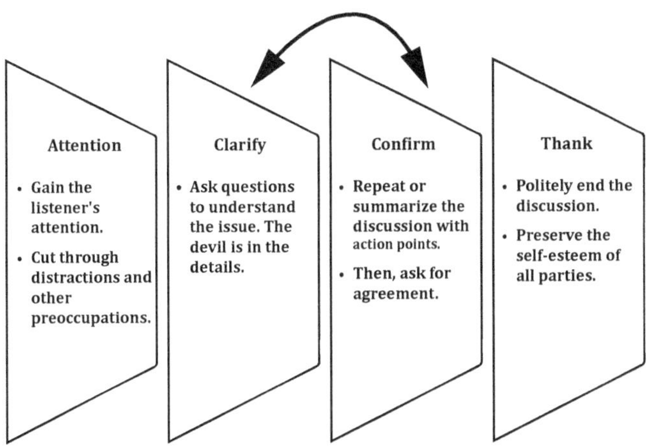

I was based in Anchorage, Alaska early in my working career. I worked at a bank, selling commercial loans. One of my remote salespeople was Brooks Berry. He was based on the beautiful Kenai Peninsula in the town of Soldotna, about three hours' drive south of Anchorage. Every day, we went through a formalized discussion ritual that later became the ACCT model. Since he worked remotely, it was important that we understood each other's needs and supported each other effectively as miscommunications were costly. Each loan document had to be prepared correctly.

This was pre-internet and pre-email.

The ACCT steps are as follows:

1. Attention. You need to gain your listener's attention at the start of the conversation. This helps prime the other party's brain to discuss the new topic(s).

When you start chatting with other people, their brains

are typically preoccupied by other matters. If you immediately start explaining a problem, you make things difficult for the other party because their brain is not yet ready. You need to allow your listener's brain to disengage and prepare to listen to your new problem.

Once both parties have gained each other's undivided attention, you can proceed to the next step:

2. Clarify. This is where you state the topic, problem, challenge, question, or change initiative that requires the listener's assistance. It's the issue's *'what'*. I recommend you also share the issue's *'why.'*

The listener asks clarifying questions to understand the issue, information, problem, or task. As a supervisor, you want to encourage your team members to ask clarifying questions all the time. You don't want them to receive your instructions silently and then say, "OK, boss." You want them to ask questions if they don't fully understand. Usually the questions are the "five wives and one husband": who, what, when, where, why, and how.

Once the problem, task, or information has been clarified, you can then get them to understand (and confirm).

3. Confirm. This step entails doing two functions:

i. Summarizing or repeating back the key parts of the issue, task, or information.

ii. Confirming with an agreement statement at the end. E.g.: "right?", "is it?", "OK?" You have confirmed successfully when the other person(s) either nods or says, "yes."

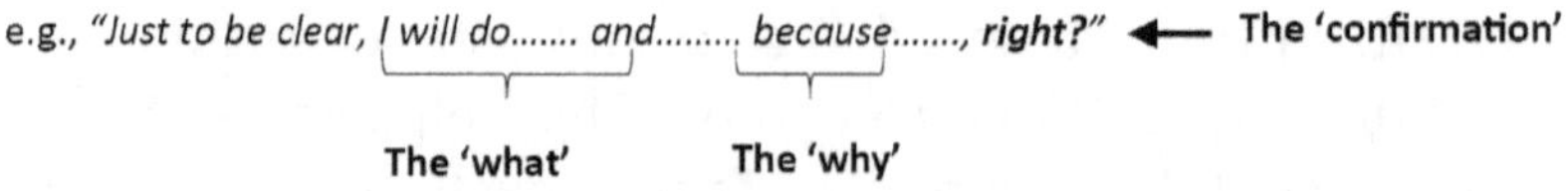

- Note: Don't make your boss, senior leader, or board member summarize or repeat back. Instead, do it for them to ensure clarity for all parties.

4. Thank. We do this to preserve working relationships and the other party's self-esteem. It also allows our brains to disengage from this conversation and move on to the next task at hand.

Note: ACCT is not limited to work situations only.

Full ACCT example

Let's see a typical Steve-to-Brooks telephone conversation. Please note that Brooks was a lonely single guy at the time. Forgive me if the conversation is long, but business runs at Kenai speed.

ACCT Step	Brooks	Steve
Attention	"Hello."	"Hi Brooks. Steve here. How's the king salmon fishing down there?"
	"Boy Steve, it's red hot. My buddy Joe was out there yesterday and caught a huge fish. You got to come down before they're gone.	Wow, that's sounds great. I've never caught a king. Yeah, I really want to go. Let's plan my trip.
Clarify	Steve, before that, our John Deere dealer here is complaining that we're taking too long to fund Meco Construction's purchase of a Caterpillar 966C wheel loader. The deal was approved two weeks ago on the 15th.	OK. How much was it?
	$100,000.	Who's the owner again?
	Wade Rose, president of Meco Construction.	Let me check, can you hold while I ask the Credit Department?
	Sure.	(2-minutes later). Thanks for holding. I talked to Tom, he said Meco's credit approval is on condition that Wade's wife signs a personal guarantee form.

	What? A personal guarantee? This is crazy. It's too much.	Brooks, they want it because Meco is a new company with only two years' experience. Plus, the wife is a corporate officer.
	Still. It's too much. Everyone down here knows Wade. He's as good as gold. Those credit guys don't know what's happening down here.	Yeah, I know. Did you read Tom's credit write-up? He asked for the wife's guarantee?
	Yes, but I stopped reading after the first sentence said it was 'approved.' I was so happy to hit my sales target this month. My mistake.	No worries. Now I've got another issue.
	What's that?	My fishing trip.
	When can you come?	What's best for you?
	How about tomorrow?	Sounds good. My boss said I could take tomorrow off. Anything I should bring?
	I've got the bait and a boat. Just bring a fishing pole and a raincoat. It's raining a lot down here. Don't worry about a hotel. You can stay at my place. What time will you arrive?	OK. I'll be there at 8:00 a.m. Thanks for letting me stay with you. I'll also bring the personal guarantee form. We can visit Meco Construction and get the wife's signature before we go fishing. When I return to Anchorage; I'll bring the signed document back to the office to get the deal funded.
Confirm	Good.	Brooks, just to confirm that we understand everything, let me summarize. 1. I'll see you at the Kenai Airport tomorrow at 8:00 a.m. 2. I'll bring my fishing pole, a raincoat, and the personal guarantee form. 3. You've got the bait and the boat handled. 4. We'll get the wife's signature before we go fishing. The next day I'll return to Anchorage with the signed form to get the John Deere dealership paid. Is that all correct?

	You got it.	Great.
Clarify	Anything else on my end?	One more thing. Please contact his wife today to prepare her for tomorrow's visit. OK?
Confirm	Steve, I'm not stupid. I'll call her as soon as we hang up.	Great. Sorry. Just wanted to be safe. Anything else on my end?
	No.	Great
Thank	Thanks Steve, we're going to catch some beautiful fish.	Thanks Brooks. I'm excited. Congrats on hitting your sales targets this month. Bye.

Did our conversations last longer than most? Maybe. To the outsider it may look like we were mentally challenged by constantly clarifying and confirming, but we just wanted to reduce the chances of miscommunicating. Did our conversations result in miscommunications, lost time, and rework? Not often. Brooks and I landed an enormous amount of business for our bank. Although he was based in rural Alaska, Brooks outperformed nearly all the other salespeople, even the ones based in major cities. One reason was because of the clarity of our communications.

In the post-COVID era, many of your team members will be remote. It's important that your remote team's instructions, needs, and challenges are well-communicated to avoid unnecessary hiccups.

ACCT's engine is Clarify and Confirm. It spins around in a circular fashion on each discussion item until each item is fully understood. I'm sure you have done it unconsciously when you think you heard someone ask for, "Fifteen." You clarify and confirm by asking, "Fifteen or fifty?"

The confirmation step is like reading the action items at the end of a formal meeting.

Clarify   **Confirm**

Use ACCT with your team to reduce miscommunications. Plus teach your team to do it with you and each other. Even with customers. Miscommunications are costly for companies, employees, and customers. They can also get you fired.

ALL organizational mistakes are caused by communication problems.

People will give all kinds of excuses to cover their mistakes and avoid blame. But if you dig, dig, and dig — you will find the problem was caused by someone not communicating something properly. I don't care if the problem is not hitting a sales target, an IT system crash, a failed new product launch, an angry customer, or a poorly maintained power system crash that disrupts cellular services for thousands of Kuala Lumpur customers for 24 hours (true story). Something, somewhere, somehow was not communicated properly from someone to someone.

A tragic example of miscommunication was the Beirut Port explosion on 4 August 2020 where 2,750 tons of highly explosive ammonium nitrate were stored in a warehouse within throwing distance of downtown Beirut. Shockingly, the ammonium nitrate was stored there since 2013. When the explosion took place, the port authorities were not surprised as they had highlighted this matter for years — but no one listened or acted. The explosion had the magnitude of between 1,000-1,500 tons of TNT and killed at least 200 people, injured about 5,000, made 300,000 temporarily homeless, and resulted in damages of 10-15 billion US dollars.[12]

Communication skills are so important. When I conduct job interviews, for any position, I evaluate ALL interviewees' communication skills. I have yet to find a job that didn't require these skills. You will not be successful as a supervisor if you cannot communicate properly: ACCT will help you.

After you assign important tasks to people, don't walk away and think that's enough. Keep a task log and follow up

---

12   "Beirut Explosion: What We Know So Far", *BBC News*, August 11, 2020, https://www.bbc.com/news/world-middle-east-53668493 (Accessed January 4, 2021).

with that person before it's completed. Tracking important tasks allows you better quality control on the final output. I'll follow-up more frequently if the task was given to a new team member. A by-product of following up, if done nicely, is a stronger relationship with your people. You will be seen as an active boss. You can also give your team the coaching that they need. By following up, I increase the chance for success which I can then pass to them credit for a job well-done. Following up leads to more happy endings.

Developing Your Team's Thinking Skills

Besides encouraging proper communication, I want my team to be a brain-powered workforce. I want their brains switched 'on.' Job security is becoming more and more precarious with the increasing usage of technology. Anyone who lacks a flexible brain is at a severe disadvantage. I want to ensure that my team (and I) have the best chance of surviving in an increasingly competitive future. One way to do this is by developing my team's thinking skills.

As a new supervisor in Malaysia, I had team members approach me and ask: "Boss, the customer is saying… And I don't know what to do. What should I do?"

I'd respond with, "I don't know."

Their faces turned white. Shock would take over. I could read their minds: "The white guy doesn't know what to do!" Silence.

Then I'd say, "What do you think you should do?"

They would respond by doing either one of two things:

1) They'd give me a lost, blank stare. It was as if this was the first time a boss had asked for their ideas. It was as if they needed to search their brain to find their thinking muscles.

or

2) They'd start to sweat. I could read their thoughts, "Boss is throwing me a trick question and trying to catch me." Then they'd say, "I don't know."

If they said they didn't know, I'd tell them to approach me once they had an idea. Eventually, I was amazed with their great ideas. They are the operational experts. They are talking with customers and doing their jobs all day, not me. I haven't done their job for a decade.

It was not easy to get people to change their old working style. They must unlearn the habit of seeing their supervisor as an oracle, or as a fount of knowledge, or worse: an encyclopedia. Most of my Asian team members took three months to adjust to the new style of problem-solving. One distrustful team member took six months before he trusted me. He was so afraid of failing! But, years later, when I see my ex-team members, one of the first things they say is, *"Steve, I liked it when you listened to our ideas."*

When they gave me their ideas, it would get my brain firing, and then I could finetune their ideas. The problem-solving solutions were of a much higher quality when we had two brains working on them. The employees also liked it. Encouraging Asian employees to share their ideas is a big problem here in Asia. Firstly, many employees are fearful to speak up. Secondly, many bosses are fearful of losing power (and 'face') by asking for their team's advice.

I call this pushing back of a question to the asker as the 'tai-chi' technique. Another way to ask their thoughts is, *"What would you suggest we do to solve this issue?"*

> **☝ Tip:**
>
> I wouldn't say, 'I don't know' to your boss, senior management, or while presenting to an audience.

An example of a team member with a switched-on brain is Vasily Arkhipov[13], an officer on the Soviet submarine B-59. During the 1962 Cuban Missile Crisis, his superior ordered him to launch a nuclear torpedo against the American surface fleet surrounding his submarine. Arkhipov, understanding the consequences of such an action, convinced his captain against this order and likely saved the world from a nuclear war. Arthur M. Schlesinger Jr., an advisor in President John F. Kennedy's administration said, "This was not only the most dangerous moment of the Cold War. It was the most dangerous moment in human history."

Communicating with Your Team as a Group

Some supervisors call themselves 'hands-off' supervisors. I call them lazy. If you want your team to succeed and achieve the needed results, you need to communicate with them daily. If you can't do it face-to-face, do it via email, group voicemail, Zoom, WhatsApp group, or whatever. You need to be seen by your team as an active supervisor. You want your team working together with a plan.

You need to show your people how you identify success. Is your team able to tell others the key 1-3 tasks that need to be successfully be done to achieve success? Can they tell others how those tasks are measured?

Here are some tips when communicating to your team or department:

- Come prepared. Anticipate their questions. Share things that are new to them. If you make the communication session a bit of a learning session, it will become more valuable.

---

13 Nicola Davis, "Soviet Submarine Officer Who Averted Nuclear War Honoured with Prize," *The Guardian,* October 27, 2017, https://www.theguardian.com/science/2017/oct/27/vasili-arkhipov-soviet-submarine-captain-who-averted-nuclear-war-awarded-future-of-life-prize (Accessed January 7, 2021).

- Express concern if they share problems. Of course, you want them to first try to solve the problem by themselves (or as a group). But some solutions may be out of their control, e.g., interdepartmental problems (you will need to help them with these). For problems that are unsolvable (e.g., a fast job promotion), sometimes the simple act of listening is all it takes.

- Highlight any operational problems you found and ask for their input first.

- Highlight good news and the results that you or others outside your department have witnessed. Publicly congratulate the team or team member who did the good deed.

- Don't end the group presentation without taking questions. In Asia, lower-level staff are intimidated by bosses and are afraid to ask questions. You need to force a question or two from them. Don't worry, once you get that first question or two, many more will flow from their mouths. If you close your presentation without taking questions, they will complain that you weren't open to them. They will blame you for their cowardness.

- Be authentic. Don't act like a Boss Lady or Boss Man. Be confident, but authentic.

- Use humor to connect with your team, especially during stressful times. Who likes to attend their supervisor's meeting? No one, so make yours a little fun. Boring sessions are unremarkable.

- If possible, start each day with a team morning chat or huddle. This only needs to be five minutes or so. It's nice to get people's heads screwed on correctly with a plan before the day starts. Often, we rush to the office (or our WFH laptop). Get to our desk, grab a coffee, and immediately start working without a plan in place. By taking an extra five minutes to plan, you will increase your team's effectiveness. It's also during the morning chats where they can raise concerns which hopefully reduces operational stress, increases productivity, and reduces miscommunication.

COVID has increased the number of virtual meetings. Usually the meetings are shorter, but you lose time setting it up and connecting everyone. Pre-COVID, office bosses could call quick informal huddles with their teams to resolve matters, but now with remote workers the meeting process has become more formalized, slower, and difficult. Communicating with your team may be your biggest challenge post-COVID. You will likely have to do more of it to combat your team members feeling less connected to the organization.

Tiny office rumors at the corporate headquarters, to remote employees, can sound like massive explosions. Remote employees can't easily see or walk around the office to get the organization's pulse. What they gain on freedom and time; they lose on connectiveness. Your team may be concerned about the viability of the organization. Will the company be able to pay my salary? Will I be retrenched? These questions cause stress which diverts people from their jobs. You will need to communicate frequently and quash such rumors, while updating them on important office matters.

At the same time, don't overcommunicate. Over communicating interrupts your team's workflow and will impede their results. Perhaps have designated communication times during your team's off-peak times? Discuss with your team to find the best balance that maintains productivity AND connectiveness. It's not easy finding the balance.

Your team members' direct impressions of the organization are formed by the quality of your communications and actions with them. If they feel they have a good boss, they will feel that they work at a good company because good companies hire good bosses.

You will need to improve your listening skills as well. Your remote team members may not share their personal and professional problems as easily as office-based teams. Listening is the only way that I know of to understand another's problems. Until they tell you, you simply don't know. You can only guess.

Communicating with Your Peers

Your peers — both from within and from without your department — will impact your team's success. It's important to build strong relationships with them, even friendships. One way is to not judge them. When we deal with peers in other departments, we can sometimes pigeon-hole them: "Finance people are slow"; "Engineering people are nerdy"; "HR people seem nice but really are two-faced" etc.

I like to run a game in my training sessions where I have learners sit at tables in groups of four people. And in each group of four, there are two teams (two people per team). I then pass out the game rules to each table. Everything runs smoothly while each table plays. The winning team then rotates to a different table. Suddenly you start to see conflict. The players in round 2 start to argue.

Little do they know that each table was given different game rules. Once they played with new teams, they are playing with teams operating by different rules. After they have rotated to three or four tables — and experienced three or four conflicts — I end the game because the conflict level gets too high. When I ask them, "How was it?"

They say judgmental things like, "Table 2 are cheaters", or "Table 3 aren't nice."

When I tell them that each table had different rules, they will usually laugh. We talk about the game's main messages: Each group of people (teams, departments, supervisors, whatever) will have their own operating rules. And most people won't change their rules to follow yours. You must adapt to theirs. And the worst thing you can do is negatively label them. It shows that you don't understand them. Others aren't bad; they're just different.

We all work in different departments and job functions. Each of us is in our own unique work silo. Silos aren't a bad thing as long as the silos communicate with each other and we understand how each silo thinks. Hopefully, by taking the time to understand them, they will understand us.

This training game has applications to other silos like gender silos, racial silos, age silos, religious silos, and others. Before we rush to judge others, we must first understand that they may be using a different set of rules, a different O/S.

Important aspects that you and your peers should understand about each other's O/S:

- What are your biggest challenges?
- What are your requirements for my team to work well with your team?
- What can I do to make it easier to work with us?
- How are you helping to deliver the organization's goals?
- How can I help your team (and you) achieve its goal?
- How can I help you achieve your personal goals here?

In *The Dictator's Handbook*[14], the authors analyze the behavior of dictators, politicians, and employees. They postulate that all three groups operate by the same rule: people want to get and retain power. And the way to do that is by building a winning coalition of allies who are categorized as 'essentials', 'influencers', and 'interchangeables.' And to keep the coalition loyal, you need to 'fund' them. For a dictator it might mean giving a new Mercedes to an essential general, a two-week overseas holiday to an influential bureaucrat, and a private meeting with an interchangeable. In a company it may involve helping an essential General Manager look good

---

14   Bruce Bueno De Mesquita and Alastair Smith, *"The Dictator's Handbook: Why Bad Behavior is Almost Always Good Politics"* (New York City: PublicAffairs, 2011).

to the CEO, taking an influential manager to lunch, and sending a friendly SMS to an interchangeable colleague.

Post-COVID, you will need to refresh your peer network. You want to stay 'in the loop' on important decisions, especially if you work remotely. If you find yourself excluded from important meetings, your influence will decrease, your opinion discounted, and your organizational value deteriorate.

As stated in Chapter 3, far too many hardworking bosses focus on their teams and minor tasks while neglecting to build an effective peer (and superior) network. Your biggest career opportunities and threats will come from these people. The richness of your network has a greater influence on your future career progression than your network with your team members. Your organizational value is determined by the sum of your knowledge, skills, attitude, results, and **relationships.**

Communicating with Your Boss

I'm writing this with the hope that you already have a good boss. Like, a boss who communicates with you often. If you have a bad boss — we will cover that in Chapter 7.

Your boss is 'essential' to develop you and increase your organizational visibility which will lead to increased opportunities. It's important that you have a good relationship with him or her and communicate often. This is especially important if you work remotely- or your boss does—post COVID.

Sometimes our bosses ask us to perform tasks that are simply not feasible. Your boss isn't asking you to do it just to do it, but s/he is getting pressure from above to get it done. It's important how you handle these difficult tasks so that you don't look like a loser.

A Pressurized Boss Story 

I like driving in the fast lane on Malaysian highways. I like it because it's less congested and safer. Often, I'll have madmen zoom up from behind me and tailgate. They aggressively flash their lights to tell me to move to a slower lane.

How quickly I move depends on my mood and whether the slow lane is heavily congested. Once I move over, I see the madman pass me at a higher speed (it's rarely a 'madwoman') — often with another F1 racer wannabe tailgating right behind him.

The same dynamic is at work when your boss pushes you.

So, the next time your boss asks you to do an impossible task, don't cowardly say, "OK, boss." Then later, when your boss asks you for the completed task, you deliver the bad news: "Sorry boss, I didn't have enough time to do it."

Your boss then explodes.

Courageous employees will tell the truth and say upfront, "Boss, I can't do it because there's not enough time." They get scolded immediately, but they avoid a horrible confrontation later.

Here's a technique to smoothly communicate 'No' to your boss (or anyone). It's called USS.

The USS Technique: How to Present Bad News[15]

USS is an easy 3-Step process that I have expanded from the original concept:

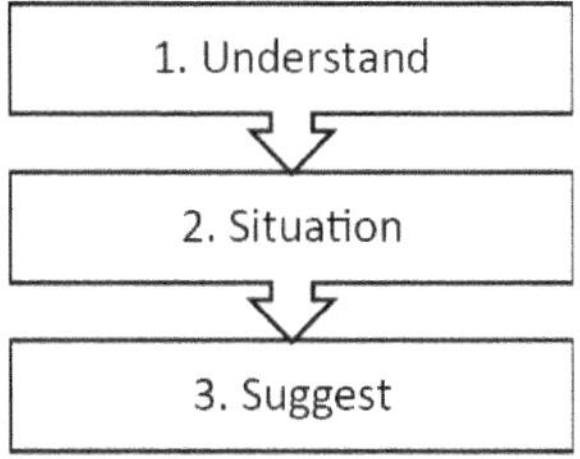

---

15   Harry E. Chambers, *Effective Communication Skills for Scientific and Technical Professionals* (New York: Basic Books, 2001), 105.

1. Understand: This shows the listener that you understand '*what*' the person wants and '*why*' (the reason). Make sure you **confirm** it!

2. Situation: After showing the listener you understand their 'What' and 'Why', you share the bad news, aka the reality. Sometimes the word 'sorry' works well here.

Before giving bad news, here are two tips:

☞ Tip 1:

Try to avoid the word "but."

☞ Tip 2:

It's wise to brace people. E.g., *"I'm sorry everyone / team / boss / Board. I have a bit of bad news..."* The advance warning prepares people for your blast wave.

3. Suggest: After sharing the bad news, **QUICKLY** suggest an alternative. Give people some hope; there are too many evil people out there who enjoy dropping giving bad news without suggestions. They drop the bad news bomb. Then shut up and smile. They watch our reaction as if they're watching a turkey roast. I've experienced these types of people when dealing with government departments.

Your suggestions will involve asking the other person for one or more of the following: more money, more time, or more people. In customer service situations, I usually offer other products, services, discounts, waivers, or an apology letter/email.

USS Example:

Imagine it's October and your boss's boss (the Chief Financial Officer) tells him or her to increase year-end profits. Now your boss is pressuring you. S/he wants your call center team to work every day in November and December — even on weekends and Christmas — till 9:00 p.m. to increase cash flow.

You know that the increased working hours will:

1. Increase overtime expenses that will bust your department's budget.

2. Increase customer complaints as no one likes calls on weekends, at night, and over the holidays.

3. Increase your teams' stress levels.

You know your teams' work environment with its people, systems, and processes. You know 100% that your boss's request is unachievable because earlier you saw a department leave report that indicated that 25% of your team will be away in both months. The leave requests have already been approved by you and your boss. You have also seen your monthly budget report and all overtime expenses have been utilized.

Your boss's request is impossible; you now need to politely tell him or her, "No."

1. **Understand:** *"Boss, I know you want us to work till 9:00 pm* (even on weekends and holidays) *because the CFO wants us to have good, year-end financial results, right?"*

2. **Situation**: *"It's just that according to the already approved leave report, 25% of the staff will be gone in November and December. Also, we have no budget for overtime."*

3. **Suggest:** *"Let me suggest that you ask the CFO for approval to increase our overtime budget for an additional RM20,000. Also, since it will be the holiday season, as an incentive to get the teams to work, I suggest we pay them twice the normal pay and not the regular 1.5 times. For those who take the offer, we should also supply free dinners so that they don't waste time leaving the office to eat. And, boss, I suggest you talk with the HR to grant us deferred-leave approval, so that we can tell our people that*

if they cancel their November and December vacations, they can still carry them forward next year. It's only fair. What do you think?"

Will your boss take your suggestions? Who knows? But hopefully s/he will see that you understand and care about the pressures s/he is under. You have shown that you see the big picture (the 'why'). You've also given your boss facts about the situation and not whined. Finally, you've given him or her a glimpse inside how your brain solves problems by offering suggestions. If I'm your boss, I'd feel good that you're on my team.

Post-COVID, organizations are looking at the bottom line even more. The old expression holds true: *"Turnover is vanity; profit is sanity; and cash is king."* Activities that don't financially contribute to the organization's survival will get more 'no's'. And you need to be able to use USS especially on your peers' non-essential requests. In the post-COVID world, you don't want your boss to forget about you. Set up a regular contact session with him or her to set goals, share your successes, and give early warnings about any future problems.

A Work Dilemma from Hell

What do you do if your boss shows up at 4:00 pm and asks you to complete Report A, Report B, and Report C by 8:00 a.m. tomorrow? The reports take you at least two hours each as you need to collate information from various departments. Now imagine you gave him or her the bad news via USS and s/he has rejected all your suggestions (more money, time, staff).

Now what?

Give the boss another type of suggestion: **prioritization.** Ask him or her to prioritize which report s/he wants tomorrow, and which ones can be delayed. Warning: don't use prioritization too often as you lose power in your boss's eyes. Still, prioritization is better than nothing if your other suggestions are rejected.

The Key Points of USS:

| 1. Understand | • Show you understand the listener's issues: the 'What' & 'Why' before giving the bad news. Confirm it! |

| 2. Situation | • Prepare them for the bad news.
• Give the bad news with facts.
• 'Sorry' is a useful word here.
• 'But' is a dangerous word here.
• QUICKLY move to Step 3 |

| 3. Suggest | • *"I suggest..."*
• Your suggestion likely involves asking for more money, people, time, alternate product/service, or boss's prioritization. |

Communicating with Senior Leaders (e.g., C-Level Folks)

Senior employees take a lot of heat from shareholders, board members, and important customers. You will also find a lot of results-orientated 'Eagles' at this level and you need to communicate with them accordingly. USS will work on them if you have good facts, suggestions and speak confidently.

Eagles are confident people and confident people respect other confident people. Your career — and possibly your boss's — often depends on how well you communicate to these people.

Here are some words that make you sound confident vs. words that make you sound weak. Please note: you just need to 'appear' confident. As the old expression goes, *"Don't let them see you sweat."*

Confident Words	Weak Words
I suggest....	Maybe we can....?
I advise...	I think we can....
I recommend...	Hopefully, we can...
I will.	I'll try.
That's a good question, let me get back to you on that.	I don't know.
Yes, we can.	I believe we can.
	I don't know if this will work, but how about....?
	I'm not sure, but how about...?

Post-COVID, your e-presentations to senior leaders (and Board) will need to be filtered to present just the most important content. Present succinctly and confidently as they won't be able to focus on heavy content and facts for long. Be well-prepared to avoid wasting their time!

Senior leaders are only human, but they are under a lot of pressure to perform. Just like any of us, they can be wrong, easily influenced, and even conned. Since they lack time, their quick decisions are often incorrect. Let me share an example of an incorrect decision that worked well for my team member because he presented confidently.

A Senior Leadership Communications Story 

Joe and I were invited to present to the 'C' level officers at a fancy resort. The senior leaders wanted an update about an initiative our department was leading. Incidentally, the initiative originated from the CEO. Joe, my team member, was the project lead on this initiative. He stood up and presented all the financial numbers, results, statistics, and whatnot. It was boring. To Joe's credit, he knew he was losing the senior leaders' attention.

He said, "Ladies and gentlemen, I'll wrap up soon as I know you all want to hit the swimming pool."

I nearly died.

Luckily the senior leaders started laughing. Joe's tone changed and he finished his presentation in a livelier fashion. Afterwards the CEO came up to me and said, "Steve, this is the kind of young people this organization needs. I want you to promote him."

I couldn't believe it.

Joe was a fairly new team member. His contribution to the team was O.K., but it wasn't sterling. If I promoted him, it would cause issues with other team members who were better performers and more senior. Still, I couldn't disobey the CEO's instruction. After discussing with my boss, I promoted Joe. But I waited six months to make it easier on the other team members.

I was amazed how the simple act of saying the right sentence to the right person could dramatically change your life.

Whenever you have a chance to present to senior management, grab it. When I first arrived in Malaysia, I was the only American in the department. I was asked constantly to present to senior leaders. Our department head would first ask my Malaysian colleagues, but they were fearful. It was a shame as it could have helped their careers (and confidence) enormously. Life is too short to live it in fear. Grab the opportunity, or someone else will. Presenting effectively to senior management increases your exposure, respect, and influence. It increases your organizational value.

> **☝Tip 1:**
>
> Before presenting to senior leaders, I will talk to one or two of them before the meeting. I ask them for advice. E.g., what the leadership team generally wants? What questions they generally ask? What are their key pressures or interests at the moment? I can then customize my presentation and reduce the number of surprises I will get on the meeting day. If I'm comfortable with that senior leader, I will even send my presentation slides or notes to him or her beforehand for feedback.

> **☝Tip 2:**
>
> Arrive early to the venue. If possible, walk around the room to visualize you and the audience. It will make you feel more comfortable. It sounds silly, but it works.

Written Communications to Senior Leaders (e.g., 'C' Level Folks)

At one job, I was responsible for collecting our customers' monthly billings. The average monthly collection was about USD 40 million. I would prepare a 10-sheet, detailed, monthly Excel collection report that I'd attach on my email for senior management to read. Inside the report were detailed comments about why we achieved this and why we didn't achieve that. After a few months of emailing it, I noticed I never got any feedback (whether positive or negative).

I concluded they weren't reading the attached report.

Senior leaders are busy people. They get lots of reports. So, I began to summarize the good parts of the reports in my monthly emails. If they wanted to read more, they could open the attachment. I didn't summarize the negative aspects—if they weren't critical-- as those were also inside the report.

Suddenly, I started getting positive feedback about what a great job my team and I were doing. My organizational influence (and power) increased. My added influence was useful for my boss and I whenever we needed their approval for extra monetary incentives (bonuses) for the department. When I resigned from the company, some of the senior leaders wanted to counter-offer me to stay.

How Well You Present Determines How Well You Succeed

As we stated at the beginning of this chapter, humans are visual creatures. God may judge us by our inner souls, but humans judge us visually. Why do beautiful young social media influencers have millions of followers? People aren't following them to read their inspiring insights. They're waiting to see their latest outfits, makeup, or sexy snaps. Or who's their next romantic partner?

In Asia, the school system is heavily focused on memorization and test taking. It's not focused on critical thinking and presentation skills. In Malaysia, students memorize the useless Beginning-Middle-Conclusion presentation model — but lack opportunities to actually present and improve their presentation skills. Their fear to present carries into their work lives.

But which senior leader (Asian or otherwise) is bad at presenting? If you want to reach an organization's highest levels, you need good presentation skills. No choice. One of the goals of this book is to help you move upward and onward. Presentation skills will help you do that.

The key to delivering a good presentation lies in good preparation. Get your facts, data, and any other materials — then practice presenting. There is no such thing as being over-prepared, but everyone will see if you're unprepared. COVID has added another complexity as now we need to learn how to confidently present and contribute during e-meetings.

I'd like to share a quick, easy, and useful presentation model. It's geared for formal presentations, but it can be used for all audiences. This includes your team, your department, and your senior leaders. It can be used for normal meetings and e-meetings.

Presentation Model: PPR (Preview-Present-Review)

It starts with a Preview of what you are going to discuss. Then Present the topic(s). Finally, end with a Review of what you presented.

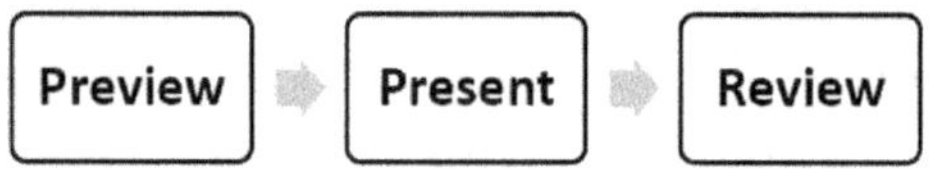

Some quick tips on each step:

Preview: Before the preview, greet the audience. Smile. I also like to gain attention by sharing a quick greeting, story, joke, thought-provoking dilemma, fact, observation, etc. This helps to disengage their brain's powers from focusing on earlier problems to now focus on my presentation.

You preview the 'what' and the 'why' of what you want to talk about. I suggest your share your conclusion here as the human brain needs things repeated a few times before it's remembered. The Preview is the most important step as your audience will judge you within those first two minutes. Project confidence and preparedness.

Present: This is the 'meat' of the presentation. I recommend not sharing more than three key issues or solutions to avoid information overload. Speak confidently when you present your 'meat'. Use confident words, tone, and body language. Present with facts and other evidence to support your recommendation or conclusion.

Review: Quickly share the key points of your presentation and re-state your recommendation or conclusion. The Review can even be a repeat of your Preview. Thank the audience and decide if you will open it up for questions.

Presenting is more than just sharing the content of your message. Usually, your audience will judge you more on 'how' you present (via their eyes and ears) than 'what' you present.

Focus on Their Eyes and Ears

Eyes:

- **Eye contact:** Share your eyes with your audience. Don't shoot your eyes like a machine gun; spend 2-3 seconds on each member. Looking them in their eyes shows confidence and builds trust.

- **Hands:** Your hands are tools to involve the audience. For serious presentations you will use restrained hand gestures. For team building and motivational speeches, you will use expressive gestures. Normal hand usage shows confidence. Stilted or no hand usage shows the opposite.

- **Body language:** For in-person presentations don't be afraid to take 1-3 steps here and there. But avoid doing it as you speak. When moving from topic 1 to topic 2 in your Present stage, you could signal the content shift by physically moving a step or two. In e-presentations doing this may be impossible.

- **Smile:** Besides using your eyes, I know of no other way to better connect with another person than by smiling. Smiling shows confidence and likeability. It increases your chance to positively influence them.

Ears:

- **Voice:** Speak in a confident, conversational tone with normal inflections. Imagine you are speaking to each person individually. People who speak in monotones sound robotic, boring, and not confident. My colleague Jude Louis says, "Your tone should be like a heartbeat. It goes up and down. It doesn't stay flat. A heartbeat is a natural sound that everyone can relate to."

I recommend memorizing your presentation (at least the key parts), especially your Preview. I don't recommend reading your presentation. Reading is boring. Instead, save their time and email or hand out your notes. In Asia, reading presentations is too common.

If you are uncomfortable memorizing, then use bullet point notes. Ensure your notes are in a large font so you don't need to bend down to read them. The PPR model will make you stand out from many other presenters. For e-presentations, you could use a second display device for your notes.

> **☝Tip:**
>
> For e-meetings and e-presentations, try to record the session and observe yourself later. How was your posture and body language? Slouching? Were you nodding when others were speaking? Did you smile when others were humorous? Did you look involved? Confident? Was your face clearly visible? Was the quality produced by your video camera and audio device good? Were your eyes incorrectly observing the audience members when they should have been looking at the camera?

How to Avoid Audience Saboteurs?

When one of my early bosses, Steve Akrish, plucked me from the lower ranks and moved me into a supervisory position, I was delighted. I didn't want to let him down for giving me the opportunity. He asked me to present a new process to the department. To increase my chances for a successful presentation, I syndicated to a future audience member. A friend. He said he'd ask me an easy question. He would act as a friendly face in the audience.

But during the presentation, this 'friend' asked immaterial, detailed questions. He wanted me to sweat and fail. I later discovered that he was upset that he wasn't chosen as a future supervisor. It was like in the movies — where the lawyer unexpectedly gets a hostile witness.

Luckily, my boss was in the audience and called the employee out for his unfair, off-topic questions. The hostile team member shut up. The presentation ended well; my boss was pleased.

You will also have saboteurs in your audiences. Even from people you trust. To reduce the risk, come overly prepared with expected questions and techniques to use if you can't answer a question — or if you get unfair, hostile questions or statements.

9 Techniques to Handle Difficult Questions and Statements

1. 'Off-line'. I use this word for difficult and complex questions that not everyone in the audience needs an explanation. E.g., "That's a great question Linda. Can I cover that off-line with you as we don't have time for it now?"

2. 'Tai-Chi'. You already have seen the 'tai chi' technique used to throw back questions to the person who asked them. It can also work to solve problems. During one departmental meeting, Faizal, was upset that when he logged into his PC each day that he was always recorded as being two minutes late. He identified that the department's PC clock was fast by two minutes, but his watch was accurate. Faizal was a detailed 'Owl'. I tai-chi'd the problem back to him to solve. "Faizal, can you be in charge of setting the department's system clock each day?" What I thought was an unimportant matter (I'm a Peacock/Eagle) was extremely important to him (as an Owl). He felt empowered with this task. He solved the problem and kept the system clock working perfectly.

3. Boomerang. Similar to Tai-Chi, this technique involves throwing an unfair question or statement back to the audience member. E.g., S/he says, "I don't like project XYZ. It's got a stupid implementation plan."

You respond, "Thanks for your comments. How would you solve it?" or, "These are the problems we're facing now… (share the 'what') because of that we created project XYZ… (share the 'why'). How would you solve it?"

People give quick, emotional <u>opinions</u> on new changes. They often won't have well-developed solutions. Complaints are easier to create than solutions. The Boomerang technique is akin to putting people in your shoes. But if they do have some good ideas, you should discuss with them 'off-line.'

4. Pause. Sometimes you will be thrown a question that takes you time to think. One strategy is to ask the person to repeat, rephrase, or give an example of that issue. Hopefully with the added time, you can coalesce your thoughts and give a good response.

In fact, this is a good technique for nearly all the questions you get from the audience. If you answer too quickly, they will think you were already prepared for that question. It also gives weight to your responses. And, more importantly, the perception that they asked a thought-provoking question makes them feel good.

5. Group pressure. This is an influencing technique you can use. Let's say one person (not a senior management leader) is dominating your presentation by asking all sorts of questions. It's getting late and you know most people want to leave. You could say, "I'd love to discuss these issues with you after this presentation, but it's getting late and I think most of the group wants to move on."

Another example, "I'm sorry you feel that way, but this was a group decision." If you want, you could mention some senior supporters or people in the group who support what you are proposing. This leads to the next technique: authority.

6. Authority. I try to avoid using authority, but there are times when you have to use it. It can save time and prevents your talk from going off-topic. In Afghanistan, I was conducting an induction program for new employees. When I came to the topic about payroll, several of the new employees said, "We dislike the company deducting taxes from our pay-slips because we don't trust our government to use the money properly."

I replied, "I understand your frustration; however, it's the law and we must follow it. I suggest you bring it up with your local politician." Although they didn't like my response, they also knew that that's life. We then moved to the next topic.

7. Audience answers. I use this technique when I get difficult operational issues that the audience knows better than I. I say, "Great question. What do you all suggest we do?" It's a 'tai chi' to the audience.

8. Smile. I smile before every presentation. It calms people. It projects confidence. It's a nice technique to diffuse conflict. I smile when I get a stupid, sometimes offensive comment that doesn't deserve much of a verbal response.

I was presenting some new HR processes at a past employer. A senior manager corrected me on my pronunciation of the word 'processes'. She said, "Steve, it's process-eez." I just smiled and said, "Thank you."[16]

16   A note on etymology: for Greek loan words that end in 'is' (thesis, stasis, proboscis), the plural form is pronounced with the eez sound. As 'process' comes from Old French, 'processes' does not require the eez sound.

9. Research. If you don't know the answer (and neither does the audience). Avoid saying, "I don't know." Instead say, "That's a great question. I'll need to research this and get back with you by (give time), OK?" Ensure you follow up with that person or group!

> ☞**Tip:**
>
> When you get a difficult question or statement (even unfair ones) — don't attack the person who raised it — even if s/he deserves it. A pack of people will defend each other, so don't attack the pack. You've heard the old saying, "He may be an idiot, but he's our idiot." Just keep cool, smile, and try your best to respond. If you're polite, the audience will usually side with you.

Influencing Skills

Influencing skills will increase your organizational power and value. This is especially important in your interactions with your peers and superiors. You need to identify who are the most important peers and superiors ("essentials") whom you need to achieve success. Influencing skills are important because they allow us to get something for virtually nothing, whereas negotiating involves trading.

You also will need to use influencing skills when dealing with your team. With today's post-COVID environment, organizations will go through many changes. Employees will be doing more and more work remotely. Some jobs will be eliminated. Some industries, like retail stores and business travel, may nearly disappear in the near term.

Post-COVID, influencing skills will take on added importance, especially if you meet each other remotely. Drinking coffee with your key organizational contacts — at the same location — may not be a daily occurrence anymore. Asking for favors isn't so easy when done remotely unless you have cultivated a strong network.

Influencing skills are easy to learn. The two writers who have written valuable books on this topic are Terry Bacon, PhD and Robert Cialdini, PhD.

Bacon's 10 Influencing Factors[17]

No.	Technique	Definition	Examples
1.	Logical persuasion	Using facts to support your view.	"I suggest we launch Product A now and Product B in six-months' time because Product A had 25% less customer complaints in our trials. It also has a 10% higher profit margin. In six months, we should have Product B's issues resolved."
2.	Socializing	Using small talk, smiling, compliments, repeating concerns, agreeing, names, laughing, and mirroring the other party to connect with them.	"Hello, my name is Steve. Abdul, I've heard a lot of good things about you and your department. I look forward to working with you to help us achieve our results."
3.	Appealing to Relationship	Using your existing relationship or commonalities to influence another.	"Siva, we're both from the same hometown. Come on friend, help me get that report out today."
4.	Alliance Building	Using peer pressure to get things done. Some may call this 'Group Pressure.'	"Team A, you should be able to complete this task by Friday because Team B and C have already completed it. I'm sure you're as good as they."

---

17   Terry R. Bacon, *Elements of Influence: The Art of Getting Others to Follow Your Lead* (New York City: Amacom, 2012).

5.	Appealing to Values	Using others' belief system to ensure they do as they say. E.g., personal, religious, family principles and beliefs. You can also GIVE people positive values (even if they don't have them). Note: People don't argue when you give positive values.	"Hugh, I know you are not a sexist person, right? (Hugh agrees). Then why did you tell Cindy that she was 'just a dumb woman'? What you said isn't consistent with what you believe. It's wrong. What's going on?"
6.	Exchanging	One-for-one. I do something for you if you do something for me. It's more negotiating.	"Team, I will treat you to dinner at the Flamingo Hotel if you exceed the target by 20%."
7.	Legitimizing	Using power to get people to do something. E.g., your job title, senior management, the law, the government, the police, company policy, etc. Some people call this 'appealing to authority.' (Note: Don't use it often).	"Zarina, company policy forbids you from billing the company for a business class air ticket because you are not senior management. I will approve the economy cost, but you will need to pay the difference yourself. Would you like to pay now or via payroll deduction?"

8.	Stating	A direct statement presented confidently for what you need. E.g., "bottom line", "final offer."	"Team, the bottom line is we need to stop the in-fighting now and work together if we want to remain the top performing team in the company."
9.	Consulting	Using the 'tai-chi' technique. Getting feedback from others to gain their support.	"Team, this is the problem… (problem's what and why explained). Now, what do you suggest we do to resolve it?"
10.	Modeling	Acting as a role model. Doing what you say, i.e., "walking the talk."	Note: I have no script here as it's how others observe you over a period of time. They will then judge whether you are a good role model or not. It's a strong influencing factor, but it takes time to prove it to them.

Of all the influencing factors, Bacon says that logical persuading is the most effective and most used factor worldwide, followed by socializing. Other effective factors include appealing to relationship, consulting, and modeling. By getting to know your team, your peers, your boss, and your senior management; you will know which influencing factors work best on them. Different people respond better to different factors.

Cialdini's Influencing Factors[18]

Cialdini has six factors, but some overlap with Bacon's.

---

18   Robert B. Cialdini, *Influence: Science and Practice* (Boston: Ally & Bacon, 2001).

I'd like to highlight and expand on two:

No.	Technique	Definition	Examples
1.	Commitment & Consistency	When people give a commitment, there is a better chance they will follow through. Consistency is similar to Bacon's 'Appealing to Values'. People like to believe that their actions are consistent with their beliefs.	"John, so I have your commitment that you will hit your target next month." The word "commitment" has a strong psychological attachment in our brains. Commitments are stronger than promises. A wedding ring has far more symbolic value than a promise ring.
2.	Scarcity	People place higher value on scarce items (e.g., money, time, food, diamonds, high-paying jobs, political positions, limited supplies, etc.). People fear losing. In Singapore they call it "kiasu."	"Choon, you are the only person getting this limited, special offer, but you need to decide by 5:00 pm today or someone else will get it."

These 12 influencing factors are especially powerful when used in combinations. Imagine you are going to use several influencing factors when presenting to the senior sales management team about purchasing a new sales tracking system.

E.g.

"Hello everyone. How's everyone today? Good job to all departments for hitting our sales target last month. I know it took detailed planning to achieve it. Let's keep it up. **(Socializing).**

"I'm here today to recommend we purchase a new sales tracking system instead of using our old manual system. The new system will help us maintain our sales lead over the competition. It will allow us to track — in real time — our customers' purchases to see what our hottest products are. We can then forecast demand. Had we used it last month, we would not have run out of Product X so early and we could have increased sales by 10% **(Logical persuasion).**

"It costs RM1m, but our CFO supports the idea because he sees the system paying off within six months **(Legitimizing).** He and the marketing head think it's a great way to get our company to the next level **(Alliance building).**

"I recommend we purchase the new sales tracking system to replace our old manual system. What do you think? **(Consulting)."**

Whether you like it or not, influencing is a critical skill that you must master. You need the support of many people — with complementary skill sets, from different teams and departments — at various organizational levels to help you and your team succeed.

Your skill at building relationships has a direct correlation on how much your employer values you. Good processes and systems are important. Achieving results is important. But if your communication and influencing skills are poor, you will fail as a supervisor.

One final point, we will all have people whom we like and dislike. It will be easier to communicate and build relationships with those whom we like; however, it's vital that you don't make enemies of those you dislike. So, avoid letting people know that you don't like them. Life and work are tough enough without making enemies.

My Chapter's Key Points:

- The ACCT model helps ensure your communications are given and received clearly. Reducing miscommunications saves time and helps you achieve your results. It also promotes critical thinking and increases communication between the different organizational levels.

- When giving and receiving instructions, the 'what' and the 'why' of the task should be shared.

- USS model is used to tell people 'No', but with a suggestion. It's better to give people bad news sooner than nasty surprises later. USS = Understand—Situation (reality)—Suggestion.

- PPR is a useful presentation tool to capture listeners' interest while logically proceeding through the presentation. I wish more presenters would use it. PPR = Preview—Present—Review.

- Your success is dependent on how well you master presentation and influencing skills. I have listed 12 influencing factors to help you deal with your team, peers, and superiors.

Now that you gained some useful communication models to lead your people, you're ready to manage them.

MANAGING PEOPLE

The secret to winning is constant, consistent management.
– Tom Landry, professional American football coach

Being a boss was the most stressful — yet most reward-ing — job I ever had. You have the world's most valuable commodity in your hands: time. You even oversee how your team members spend their time. Will you use it to mold them into creative-thinking employees or into non-thinking sol-diers? How you use that time will determine the kind of im-pact you leave on them.

Are you a Manager or a Man Ager? Does your team see you as a fair or unfair boss? Do you foster a fun, creative work environment (when feasible)? Or do you create a work envi-ronment that feels like a torture chamber?

Many people (including myself) dislike the words "super-visor" or "manager." They much prefer "leader," but as we dis-cussed in Chapter 1, all these roles do essentially the same thing. They supervise, manage, and lead (you can use other verbs here) to get people to achieve results. And how well you handle your team (and the results you achieve) will de-termine whether you are a great boss—or not.

In this chapter, we will discuss the best ways to supervise people from different generations; how to manage top, mid-dling, and poor performers; how to manage multi-cultural teams; and 16 ways of building a motivational work environment.

Now let me ask you a question. Be honest. Do you like people telling you what to do?

I'd say, "No."

Working in an organization is about selling your freedom and time in return for money and security.

This is the basic equation:

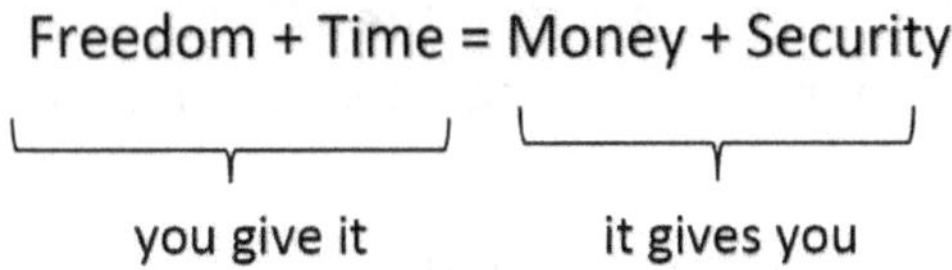

Of course, you give additional things like commitment, values, attitude, skills, etc. And the organization gives you perks like its values, stock options, workspaces, PCs, maybe even healthcare, lunches, and foosball in the break room. But the basic equation is the same. In the post-COVID context, however, the amount of job security has lessened while freedom (and time) may have increased.

If you believe that most people don't enjoy taking orders, then you're on your way to becoming a better boss. Knowing that many people have anti-boss attitudes will make you more sensitive when giving orders.

Starbucks has their method of giving instructions. Their supervisors are taught not to give orders, but to give requests:

- *"Vanita, could you please clean the expresso machine as it's getting close to closing time?"*

- *"Kevin, could you help Steve at the cash register because he's new on the job?"*

Such a sensitive supervisory style builds closer and more cooperative teams in their outlets. It also helps reduce staff turnover — the big enemy of F&B businesses. They must be doing something right as I continue to see a Starbucks on just about every street corner.

Supervising Different Generations

Management experts tell us that we must speak to Baby Boomers one way, to Gen X in another, to Gen Y in another, and to Gen Z in another. They make it sound like interpersonal communication between generations is like walking in a minefield. Or like visiting a foreign country where the locals can't speak any English at all, and you've got to learn their language(s).

I disagree.

Throughout human history, we have been communicating inter-generationally for eons. I'm sure we got it wrong sometimes. But overall, we humans have been able to communicate. If we weren't good communicators, we wouldn't have a current world population of 7.8 billion. But today we label people: Gen X, Y, or Z? Do you really think that intergenerational miscommunication is a recent phenomenon?

In the 4th century B.C.E., Aristotle wrote, "[Young people] are high-minded because they have not yet been humbled by life, nor have they experienced the force of circumstances... They think they know everything, and are always quite sure about it."[19]

I agree that our thought patterns are partially defined by our chronological age, but I disagree that we can't communicate well intergenerationally. I divide employees into roughly three age groups: the young, the middle-aged, and the senior employees.

HR people will roll their eyes at these terms. They will define them as new careers, mid-careers, and late-careers (near retirement). Or HR will fall back on the Gen labels. But who cares?

---

19   Quoted in Amanda Ruggeri, "People Have Always Whinged About Young Adults. Here's Proof," *BBC Worklife,* October 3, 2017, https://www.bbc.com/worklife/article/20171003-proof-that-people-have-always-complained-about-young-adults (Accessed June 16, 2020).

Psychologists list the different needs and fears we have throughout our life stages. Young people have different needs than middle-aged people and seniors. And vice versa. As supervisors, we need to understand peoples' general needs based on their grouping.

Possible general needs include:

Young employees	Middle-aged employees	Senior employees
• Gain work experience	• Impact the organization	• Share knowledge
• Gain basic skills & training	• Achieve mastery level & advanced training	• Coach or train others
• Receive positive praise from immediate boss	• Move up	• Do projects I enjoy
• Gain work friends, meet a potential spouse	• Formal recognition & awards	• Learn completely new things
• Casual environment	• Connect with senior management	• Recognition as the 'go-to expert'
• Team activities	• Influence organizational strategies / goals	• Health
• Business travel	• Lead teams, projects, & chair meetings to gain status, influence, power	• Set organizational strategies and goals

The experiences we gain as we age aren't limited to knowledge and skills. We also gain emotional experiences. As a young person, I was more emotional than I am now (at 61). The young Steve was more sensitive to criticism and far more defensive than the mature Steve. Now if you criticize me, I'll probably agree.

A middle-aged employee can be severely affected if s/he is passed over for a promotion. They can also be greatly affected by retrenchments as they likely have car loans, house loans, and children's tuition payments. Whereas if an older employee is retrenched, s/he may not always be as severely affected.

It's important to anticipate what different people value before giving them instructions, feedback, and appraisals. And it's not easy. Just because people are at a certain age, it doesn't mean they will have the same general needs of others in the same age group. The key is knowing your people and asking them about what motivates them.

Managing Your Top Performers (Stars)

It's important to know who's great, who's good, and who's not that great. Let's discuss how to supervise an assortment of people at varying levels of knowledge, skills, and attitudes.

Stars are your top performers. They are the people who help you exceed the target. As top performers, they can act as role models and coaches to any team members with performance issues. When one or more of your Stars are away, the team suffers. Whatever you do, don't treat them unfairly and give them a reason to be pissed at you.

Stars will usually demonstrate leadership capabilities. The best way for you to leave a legacy at your organization is to enhance your Stars' leadership skills. Some of these people may even rise higher than you at the organization or at another. Some will help you in your future, provided you have been a good boss.

Some of my lesser performers complained that I had favorites in my department. My response was, "You're damn right. You can also be my favorite if you perform at (the Star's name) level." Stars are my favorites. I give them more freedom, more time, first choice at taking leave, whatever. I forgive their mistakes more easily as they have often covered for mine. Many of my Stars will be next in line to be promoted. I spoil them rotten.

Your Stars become your "Mini-Me's": People who support what you are doing in the department or team. Use them to get the rest of the team to buy into your new change initiatives. I've seen professional sports players get yelled at by their coach. And the same players yell back at the coach. They show the coach no respect. The coach is probably older and makes far less money than the young player. But, when that same youngster gets yelled at by the team's Star, boy, things change.

Your Stars help build the culture you want. They attract others who want to be like them. Influencing techniques show us that Group Pressure and Modeling move people to action. Why not have a high-performing group pressure culture within your team that other team members want to model?

Q: What do you do if your Star is better than you?

A: You could do three things:

1. Hurt the person and get the Star resentful of you (and get other Stars pissed at you) and watch your team's results deteriorate.

2. Promote him or her.

3. Assign additional work responsibilities (non-promotional).

I interviewed a candidate that I could see would be a future Star. He was more skilled than me in certain respects. He gave an impressive job interview; his superior intelligence was evident. I could have felt threatened and immediately rejected him, but that's unethical. Instead, I hired him, and he eventually replaced me. Was I bitter? At first, yes. But I moved into a new department that taught me new skills and gave me more contacts and greater responsibilities. I also got a great boss. From that new job, I was able to start my own business. By hiring the Star, I had freed myself to develop additional skills to increase my value.

My Star has since left our old employer and worked in senior positions at some great companies. He's unleashing his potential. He's also a friend.

Bottom line: Don't treat your Stars unfairly or they will leave your team. Of course, they may get upset at you once in a while, but as long as you are a fair boss, you should be OK. You and your organization need the Stars more than they need you.

Be aware that Stars don't stay forever. There is a talent war for them; your goal is to hold them for as long as you ethically can. With the advent of COVID and remote work, your Stars will get headhunted from more competitors, even from overseas competitors. The key retention asset that your organization has to keep them is YOU.

Managing Your Average Performers (Steady Eddies)

These are the people we often ignore. They aren't your Stars, but neither are they your problem employees. They are usually the silent majority who do an honest day's work with a positive frame of mind. They might not help you exceed the target, but they do help you meet the target.

Unfortunately, sometimes it's difficult to raise their performance level. They are typically in a comfortable routine. They have experienced a certain level of success by maintaining their current performance level, and many don't want to change. Some may even be satisfied with their lives and uninterested in advancing in their careers.

If you move more Steady Eddies to become Stars, your team and department will achieve better results. Perhaps achieve results that no other supervisor has ever achieved before with them.

Managing Your Poor Performers (Slugs)

Poor performers take up a lot of your time. But first you need to determine if the poor performance is due to a 'skill' or a 'will' problem.

- **Skill Problems:**

These are the easiest to solve. It's not their fault if they're performing poorly. Perhaps HR and you didn't properly interview and access their skills? Or your organization didn't give them the required training, coaching, or tools. For these people, you need to work with them and design a development plan to upskill them. Treat them fairly and give them a chance to succeed.

During the development plan, check with them on their progress. Assign a Star to be part of their support network to help them succeed. Express confidence in them. When they do improve, give them positive feedback.

If their skill problems don't improve after an intervention, then consider a job downgrade, a transfer, or a termination. Most jobs can't be done by everyone.

- **Will Problems:**

Although you have built a performance-based work environment, some people will be tempted to become slackers. Maybe some are immune to the team's group pressure, even from the Stars? To some people, earning a paycheck without working is heaven.

On a recent flight from Cyprus, I sat next to a Canadian airman who had been in the Canadian air force for nearly 20 years and was approaching retirement. He was a plane mechanic. I asked him what he planned to do upon retirement.

He said, "Join a rural Canadian police department."

What? That was an odd response.

I asked, "Why not join an aeronautical company and do something you know and get paid more?"

He said, "Then I'd have to work."

He was afraid that if he worked in a private company his laziness would be discovered and he'd soon be fired. Whereas he could hide his future poor performance easier by working as a cop in rural Canada.

But Slugs aren't limited to Canada.

I was speaking with a manager at a U.S. embassy. He said one of his Slugs, a fellow American, sat at his PC all day taking online courses to get a master's degree. He said that he couldn't threaten him with termination because the ambassador would have to prepare a report that would be sent back to Washington D.C. The embassy's leader didn't want that kind of attention. Clearly, this wasn't a performance-based work culture. The ambassador lacked courage.

Our teams must succeed if we want to keep our jobs. Unfortunately, our Slugs are a barrier to our success. You need to ensure that your work environment doesn't reward poor performance. Build a work environment that makes poor performance uncomfortable. You want Slugs to know that not performing is more stressful than performing. I know it's tough to change their complacency. Habits get ingrained, but you need to highlight poor performance quickly and frequently — and keep detailed records of it.

Napoleon supposedly said, "There are no bad soldiers, only bad officers." I partially disagree. There are bad soldiers. You upskill the soldiers with 'skill' issues and you remove any roadblocks. If they still can't perform, get rid of them.

If you have bad soldiers who have been in the military (or your organization) for years, and you didn't do anything about it, then yes, I agree with Napoleon. If this describes you or your organization, you'll soon face your own Waterloo if you don't act fast.

Make Slugs aware of the effects of their poor performance. I keep the poor performance (and good performance) reports visual. I like reports with people's names on them, publicizing their individual and team performance. I share them. At one employer, I posted the department's daily performance statistics, by name, in the pantry.

Post-COVID and with the rise of remote work and additional monitoring tools, it will likely be easier to quantifiably track poor performance and pin responsibility on its cause. You may see some of your past Slugs greatly improve their performance, though they may still blame IT equipment, internet connections, and other technologies for their poor results.

At another employer, all team members log-in to their daily system and see their month-to-date performance versus others in that same department. This works well in quantitative jobs like sales, fault reporting, debt collections, and contact centers.

Same as for 'skill' problems: if the Slugs' 'will' problems don't improve, then start planning a job downgrade, transfer, or termination.

"The Dental Office"

Nobody likes visiting the dentist. But the longer we postpone it, the more serious the problem becomes. I use the "dental office" concept to deal with poor performers. It works well in jobs that have quantitative performance goals. Let's use an example of a salesperson who must achieve RM 100,000 in sales per month. It could also be used for a technician that has to solve X number of faults per day or month. If that person misses his or her target, s/he needs to meet in their supervisor's office (the 'dental office').

At this private meeting, the team member explains why s/he missed the monthly target. Notes are taken and a plan is agreed on. The team member is wished good luck and the supervisor expresses confidence that this will be a one-off failure. The supervisor also alerts the team member what will happen if this is repeated. A visit to the department head, for example.

If the team member misses the target on the next month, escalate the matter to senior management. If this goes on for another month, maybe to HR. You want the slug to know their poor performance is attracting bad attention — and this will not result in a happy ending.

Of course, don't escalate if the employee has legitimate reasons for the continual poor performance. Legitimate reasons include maternity leave, vacation, critical illness, or other such reasons. However, it's still a good idea to have a pleasant chat about the impact their absence had on the department.

The dental office ensures that poor performance is highlighted, tracked, discussed, and extinguished early. Prevention is better than cure.

Visiting the dentist is never fun, but ignoring poor performance is worse as it will spread to others. Your people are watching you on how you handle it. Finally, the dental office removes surprises when people are demoted, transferred, or fired (after you have coached, trained, and warned them). It forces communication.

Managing People Based on Their Strengths: The Fiddler Crab Principle

I'm a firm believer that you should develop your people's strengths until they become superstars. I'd much rather have fiddler crabs on my team than puny rock crabs. As a child, I spent my summers at my grandparent's seaside home near Bremerton, Washington. At low tide we'd prowl around the beaches and turn over rocks. We'd find tons of puny rock crabs underneath. Their pinches didn't hurt much.

But I'd see fiddler crabs that lived in other parts of the world on television. You know, those crabs with one puny arm and one huge claw. If they pinched you with their huge claws, it would hurt like hell. They can even draw blood.

We are taught to turn dogs into cats and cats into dogs in the corporate world. HR wants us to close people's will and skill gaps. This sounds fine in theory, but not all gaps can be closed in practice. A person who has presented many times and dislikes it shouldn't be forced to improve his or her presentation skills. A person who has done accounting and dislikes it shouldn't be forced to do it. A person who has sold before and dislikes it shouldn't be forced to sell.

Throughout my career, my bosses have tried to make me into a more detailed person. I'm sorry, that's just not my strong suit. Ask my wife. My desk is a mess. I believe that if you force me to become more detailed, I'll miss the big picture. You are hobbling my strengths. Instead, I wish I had bosses who allowed me to further develop my big-picture-thinking skills. Make me into the largest, big-picture-thinking fiddler crab you have ever seen.

Your team consists of people with various strengths and weaknesses. You need to realize that you can't close all the gaps. And your people will be against closing some of those gaps, too. Instead, get to know your people and decide which gaps are closeable and which ones you can transfer to others or accept at a lower quality standard. Then, focus on strengthening their strengths. Build powerful fiddler crabs. Your people will thank you since you're allowing them to improve an area they enjoy. You are developing them into an expert in their field.

John Maxwell believes that we should let our people focus their time on the following:

80 percent of the time they work in their strength zone;

15 percent of the time they work in their learning zone;

5 percent of the time they work outside their strength zone; and

0 percent of the time they work in their weakness zone.[20]

Supervising a team is a balancing act. You need to give tasks to those who are best at that task. Don't focus on closing all the gaps if the payoff isn't there. You can't make a dog into a cat.

COVID-19's Effect on Managing Different Levels of Performance

COVID has affected all our team members. You may find some top performers who 'crashed' during the pandemic, while maybe some 'Steady Eddies' excelled. Analyze who were your team members that still contributed during the crisis's darkest moments. Don't waste this crisis opportunity as it teaches us a lot. Ensure you thank and reward those team members who shined under stressful conditions.

Managing in a Multicultural Context

In Malaysia, I ran a large department with multiple races and religions. I was the only white person. I found it no different than working in the U.S. In both countries we cared more about performance than race.

One way to see if there is racism and sexism practiced in companies is through the ethnic and gender composition of their supervisory teams. If the supervisory teams are solely of one race or gender, often their boss will be of that same race or gender. For me, I promoted employees based on their performance and attitude. And I found these criteria in all races and genders.

---

20   John C. Maxwell, *The 5 Levels of Leadership: Proven Steps to Maximize Your Potential* (New York: Hachette Book Group, 2011), 162.

Nowadays, companies compete worldwide. With the rise of China, more and more businesses will have to compete against it. And I fully support fair competition. It makes every business better and benefits consumers.

We also have to worry about the rise of automation and AI. These technological breakthroughs will disrupt many jobs. Technology companies are some of the richest on the planet, especially post-COVID. Bloomberg News reports that Japan's second largest firm is Keyence, an industrial robotics maker that is worth USD100 billion. Its market value has tripled since 2016. Its founder, Takemitsu Takizaki, is Japan's third richest person.[21]

Supervisors need to harness the power of having a multi-ethnic workforce to compete. Racist and sexist supervisors will fail. People from different cultures and genders don't necessarily think like you. But I guarantee that you will overcome most cultural and gender issues if you treat them with respect and fairness.

Still, you may have exceptions.

As a college student I spent my summers processing salmon in Bristol Bay, Alaska. 18 hours a day, 7 days a week. The red salmon run lasts for just one month. One of my colleagues was an Alaskan tribal native. He was a great worker — when he showed up. Some days he didn't arrive. He was unable adapt to the daily work culture. Or maybe he did not get a full explanation of the company's work culture during the on-boarding process. He was soon fired.

However, we had top performers from the Athabaskan, Yakima, and Flathead tribes coming from Alaska, Washington state, and Montana respectively. My work experience was enriched by learning about their different cultures. At the same time, I discovered we aren't so different after all.

---

21   "#3 Takemitsu Takizaki", *Forbes*, January 29, 2021, https://www.forbes.com/profile/takemitsu-takizaki/?sh=782d6105439c (Accessed January 30, 2021).

Building a respectful, fair, performance-based work culture, and communicating the right values is always a work in process. Here are some tips for supervising multicultural teams:

1. During your team's various cultural holidays, dress up in their traditional costumes. You may think you look stupid (and maybe you do), but the people from that ethnicity love it. I'd dress up for the various Chinese, Malay-Muslim, and Indian-Hindu celebrations.

2. Ensure your team has a small budget to celebrate their major festivals. If you lack the budget, at least recognize them verbally.

3. Learn a bit of the language, culture, and religion from each ethnic group.

When you learn a bit of another's culture, you are showing that you spent time learning. The benefits are enormous. You connect deeply with them as it's something they have known since birth.

REMOTE Management Aid

I wanted to share with you a mnemonic aid that may help you if you manage remote workers. You will likely have to customize it for your environment. Rene Villa is a San Francisco based senior IT manager specializing in big data. He has been managing people remotely for over 20 years. At one employer his boss said, "Your team is one our best. They love you and you're not even here. How do you do it?"

Rene replied, "That's probably why they love me."

He discovered successful remote teams require three conditions:

1. Promote an environment of trust between the team members and the supervisor.

2. Develop your team's independent problem-solving skills as you won't always be around.

3. Encourage your team to build an extensive network of people to contact to help them problem-solve. The network is both within and outside the organization.

Rene's acronym REMOTE summarizes the key components of his remote management style:[22]

Review

He recommends bi-weekly 30-minute video conferences for experienced employees and weekly video conferences for less experienced or new employees. The initial chat should include analyzing the employee's skill level, understanding his or her work preferences, and listening to their career goals. You need to consider how you will support their goals.

Encourage

As you get to know you employees better, encourage them to challenge themselves to take on more complex projects to grow their skill sets and confidence. It may require the employee looking outside your team or department to gain the needed skills or knowledge. S/he may need to attend external or internal training. Or, s/he may need to contact internal subject matter experts to get the needed new skills or knowledge. From time to time, you may be required to make some of these internal connections.

Motivate

Encourage your remote employees' independent problem-solving skills to overcome roadblocks. In your regular video-conferencing meetings, understand their challenges and brainstorm solutions. Don't provide

22   Rene Villa, "A Six Phased Leadership Approach for Managing Teams Remotely," LinkedIn, August 27, 2020, https://www.linkedin.com/pulse/six-phased-leadership-approach-managing-teams-remotely-rene-villa/   (Accessed August 27, 2020).

the solutions yourself. Instead, ask for their solutions first. But do let you team know you are there to support them.

Observe

Observe both the quality of their work and the quality of their interactions with others, then provide coaching. Remote employees will produce good work, but sometimes at the expense of their interpersonal relationships. Perhaps they didn't communicate to their teammates or others as nicely as they could have to produce that work?

Trust

Show that you trust them to work independently and make the right decisions. Trust works best when you allow mistakes. Without trust, your employees won't feel supported and will soon lose confidence in themselves (and you). Fear creeps in and prevents them from developing into their true potential.

Expand

Like changing a flowerpot when a flower grows larger, you need to expand your employees' roles and responsibilities. Take your time here as each employee's skills, knowledge, and confidence increases at different rates. Nor will all embrace their roles' expansion. You will need to work with their different levels of readiness for the new changes.

Motivating the Team

This is a difficult topic. A lot of what 'experts' write about motivation is simply crap. I don't believe anyone can motivate another. So, don't try to motivate your team. Only they can do that.

Organizations pay a lot of money to have external speakers come and motivate their people. To me, it's a con job. I don't enjoy external speakers telling me that I can reach for the stars, walk on hot coals, or slay dragons. I already know that. If I'm a good supervisor, my people should already know that too.

I don't want my people to be externally motivated by external speakers. I want them to be internally motivated by our team's work environment and themselves as then it's self-perpetuating. If the motivation source is external, once that source is gone the 'motivation' disappears within a week. We revert to our old selves. Just like a fad diet.

If you need an external person to motivate your people to do their jobs, then something is wrong at your workplace. Are the organization's supervisors so inept that they need external, high-priced speakers to motivate their people to do their jobs?

Motivational speakers remind me of those external organizations that come into an undeveloped country and build a high-tech hospital. Then then walk away. The locals can't maintain the hospital and after a while the hospital is converted into low-cost housing or a place to house farm animals.

I believe that you can build a motivational environment, but it's up to your people if they want to partake in that environment. You can't force motivation. Also, you yourself need to be motivated before you can build that environment. Ideally, you have selected, hired, and retained top performers who already are motivated. For these people you just need to ensure you don't de-motivate them.

I aim to create a work environment that is performance-based, diverse, creative, fair, and fun. I'm hoping that the work culture that results from these factors will lead employees to motivate themselves. But I can't guarantee you that they will be motivated.

Motivation is a choice. When employees complain to me that they are demotivated and want me to motivate them, I respond, "So do I!" I tai-chi the problem back to them, "What do you suggest to motivate us both?"

Saiful's Story

Saiful was a poor to average performer. He was doing a job that he didn't like for far too long. But suddenly his performance turned around and he became one of the department's Stars. I congratulated him for the positive change. I asked him what had happened.

He said that his wife was divorcing him and taking their two children. He realized he needed to be a better performer to achieve the monthly bonuses and provide a better life for his children. He also implied that his wife left him because she deemed him to be a loser.

Saiful won our department's 'most improved' award that year.

He remained a top performer and became one of my favorite team members. He's still a friend. But I didn't motivate him; it was his choice. All I did was provide a work environment that paid monthly bonuses to reward him for making that choice.

Core Factors in a Motivational Work Environment

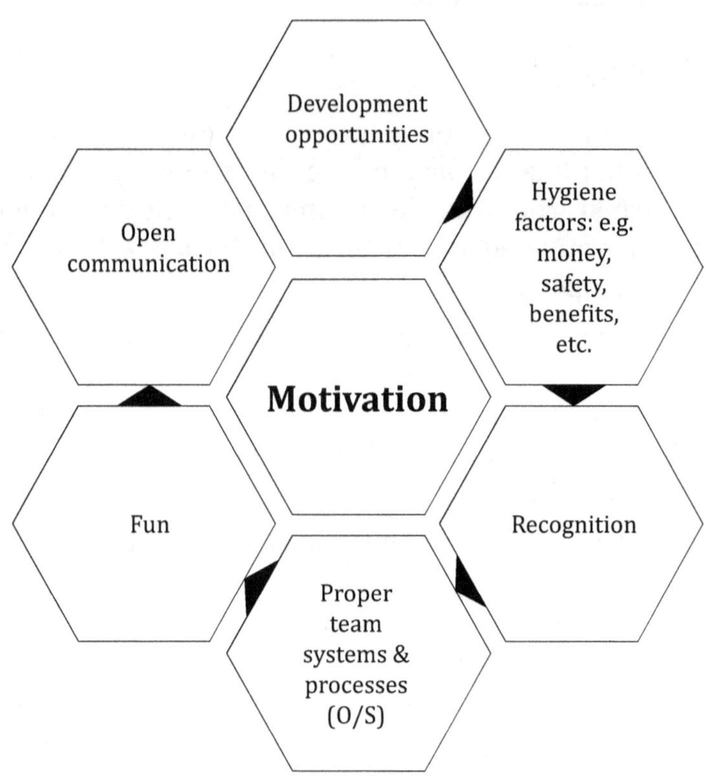

16 Ways to Build a Motivational Work Environment:

1. Share the 'Why'

We usually share the 'what' when we talk to our team members, but when we share the 'why', we are sharing the big picture of what we want to achieve. People feel motivated if they become part of something bigger than themselves. Although each person's job is just one tiny piece of the mosaic, you increase the team's motivation by sharing the big picture of how all their pieces fit together. Sharing the 'why' gives the job meaning.

2. Good Supervisors Working in a Positive Work Environment (O/S)

The polling company, Gallup, took ten years to collect interview data on two million employees and 300,000 business units.[23]

> "The results confirmed something Gallup had seen before: a company's productivity depends, to a high degree, on the quality of its managers.
>
> What no one saw coming, however, was the sheer size of that correlation — something Gallup calls 'the single most profound, distinct and clarifying finding' in its 80-year history. The study showed that managers didn't just influence the results their teams achieved; they explained a full 70% of the variance. In other words, if it's a superior team you're after, hiring the right manager is nearly three-fourths of the battle.
>
> No other single factor, from compensation levels to the perception of senior leadership, even came close."

If your people have courageous and ethical supervisors and colleagues — who do their jobs in a performance-based, fair capacity — people appreciate it. You will also attract and retain better talent. People will even reject more lucrative external job offers if they like and respect their current boss and colleagues. Your people's direct supervisors have more influence on them than you or even the CEO.

The Economist reports that COVID has changed the traits of a successful boss. Office workers still value bosses who are confident and charismatic. But remote workers value bosses who are:

---

23   Sam Walker, "The Economy's Last Best Hope: Superstar Middle Managers," *Wall Street Journal*, March 24, 2020, https://www.wsj.com/articles/the-economys-last-best-hope-superstar-middle-managers-11553313606?mod=article_inline (Accessed January 4, 2021).

"organized, productive and facilitate connections between colleagues. In a post-COVID world, companies will have to place greater emphasis on retaining and promoting leaders who have these skills."[24]

Although your work environment is performance-based and competitive, it doesn't mean it isn't fun. Encourage your supervisors and their teams to enjoy their jobs and each other while achieving the company's goals.

3. Win

Nothing builds motivation and teamwork better than winning. Winning makes people feel proud. They will even overlook other weaknesses and faults within your team (and you) if they win. Working in organizations is about making money, providing value, and winning. Employees will more easily forgive a tough boss who wins versus a friendly boss who loses. On the other hand, a series of losses can destroy a team. Celebrate wins! Even small ones, even tiny ones.

4. Remove Barriers

These could include fixing poor equipment, IT systems, PCs, bottlenecks from other departments, senior management intrusions, budgetary issues, and other matters that interrupt a team's workflow. Allowing your team members to work uninterruptedly allows them to produce more at a higher level of quality. It allows people to get "in the flow." When people are "in the flow", creativity and job satisfaction increase.

Micromanagers stop flow. Supervisors need to remove barriers and get their teams the tools they need to succeed, then get out of the way and allow them to achieve their goals with creativity and ingenuity. This is especially relevant post-COVID.

---

24   Erica Brescia, "At Software Firms, Many People Already Worked from Home," The *Economist*, November 17, 2020, https://www.economist.com/the-world-ahead/2020/11/17/at-software-firms-many-people-already-worked-from-home (Accessed January 4, 2021).

5. Fix HR Mistakes

Whenever I join a new department, I ask HR to provide me with everyone's salary. I do this for a few reasons. In one report I received, I could see that a Star — a quiet, middle-aged person with many years' experience — was at a wrong pay grade and job title. She had been underpaid and mis-designated for two years. I highlighted this error to HR, who fairly readjusted her pay and gave her a job title appropriate to her experience and contribution.

In another report, I found that a Slug had been paid an extra incentive by mistake. I deleted that. Another report showed that a Steady Eddie had one of the highest salaries in the department. I spoke with him about how he will need to increase his workload to justify that salary.

If you see your team is paid below-industry average, you need to fight for your people and highlight this matter to HR. Ideally, I want my team's salaries to be above industry average.

The benefits of paying more are many:

a) Attract and retain better staff. There's a talent war for top performers. You don't want to lose your Stars. Also, retaining staff saves money in recruitment, headhunter fees, and training. If you pay below average, your team members will use valuable time looking for jobs outside. Finally, paying more attracts a better-quality staff which allows me to save time managing poor performers.

b) Esprit de corps. Team's spirit increases when they see themselves as having more value than comparable companies. In addition, just like professional athletes, we want Stars and Super Stars on our teams so that we can learn, improve, and win more. This leads to a better work environment. Netflix pays above market rates for its talent for this very reason.[25]

---

25   Reed Hastings, Netflix's CEO, has uploaded an excellent document (in slide format) about their organization's strategic values. *"Freedom and Responsibility Culture* (Version 1), 2009, www.slideshare.net/reed2001/culture-2009?next_slideshow=1 (Accessed September 15, 2020).

c) Stressor. The higher salaries act as a stressor to get people to perform more. Stress is good. Life is about stress. I thank God each day for my stress. This isn't about being a ruthless bastard to your staff. In the book *Good to Great*, Jim Collins describes it better. It's not about being 'ruthless'. It's about being 'rigorous.'

d) Valuable human capital. Besides further strengthening their skills and knowledge, employees forge deeper relationships with each other, other teams, other departments, and customers when they work in the same company for a long time. They become more valuable, experienced, and make less mistakes. Their work quality, quantity, and speed increases.

6. Develop People via Special Projects

I reward my Stars with special projects to stretch their brains. It may or may not be related to their current job, but it is likely related to a skill that I have seen in that person. For example, Azlin was a Star who also enjoyed technology. My department bought a new IT system and the vendor asked for some in-house testers. My testers would work with the vendor so that they could better understand our system requirements. The end-result was a new system designed for our unique needs. Azlin learned new IT skills, met new people, gained more recognition, and increased her value.

Special projects can include designing new processes, creating new training programs, designing new reports, or even giving tours to departmental visitors. I've seen some Stars who do the special project so well, and with such enjoyment—like Azlin—that they change their careers to follow that new skill.

Environmentalists tell us that the only constant in nature is growth. And just like any plant, most of your team members want to grow. You need to provide your Stars with these opportunities—like special projects—or they will grow elsewhere.

7. Develop People via Internal or External Training, Conferences, and Conventions

Although the best training and learning environments are on-the-job, sometimes it's worthwhile to have team members attend external training events, conferences, or conventions. These learning events let employees hone their skills by showing them how others do similar jobs. Your people can network within the field. It's fun and recharges their batteries.

In the past, external training was focused on the younger and newer employees, but with the shelf-life of education degrees and qualifications shortening, older employees will need to upskill themselves if they want to keep their jobs and higher salaries.

8. Develop People via Departmental Transfers

If you have a good network of peers and superiors at your organization, consider transferring your Stars to each other's departments. The cross-training is a great motivational factor where they can learn new skills.

In addition, you can also transfer Slugs to departments that people do not wish to go to. This is a wonderful motivating factor for Slugs to improve their results. I had a great peer relationship with, Manju, who ran the Customer Service contact center. She would transfer her Slugs to my department, Collections, and I'd transfer mine to hers. Once her Slugs joined my department, all became Steady Eddies and one even became a Star! These people didn't need to be fired. When people perform poorly, often it's due to poor job fit. If they find the right job and work environment, they can succeed.

9. Develop People via Internal Job Promotions

Too many companies promote from outside. They do this for positions at all levels, not just at the senior level. What kind of signal does this send to your employees?

Answer: You're not good enough!

If your employees aren't good enough, then you're also saying that your supervisors aren't good enough because they didn't develop their people well enough. And if your supervisors aren't good enough, then your senior leaders aren't good enough either. It's sending a horrible message both within and outside the company.

I have hired outside people for managerial jobs. Sometimes I've got a great person, other times a lousy one. For the majority of job promotions, I recommend you choose an internal candidate. It shows that you have confidence in your people.

Most organizational jobs don't require its employees to perform major brain surgery. Most jobs are learnable if the person has half a brain and a good attitude. I've found that most organizational jobs can be learned in 6-12 months. No matter what HR Recruitment says, most organizational non-technical jobs aren't complex.

Sure, outside new hires may say they have special skills and experience, but that doesn't mean that they will be immediately successful in your organization. How often does HR and others actually test people to determine if they're as good as they say? Or do a detailed check on their past employers? We usually only know if they are truly good after they're hired. It can also take the outside new hire months to learn how to fit into the new organization.

Promoting people from outside reminds me of meeting my son's schoolteachers at the start of each school year. The teachers will lively present how much they like kids, what a great teacher they are, about how much they love the subject they teach, etc., etc. I feel like I'm being sold a used car.

But I won't know for sure if they're good until a month after the school year starts. So, I wait and ask my son, "Hugh, who are your good teachers and who are the lousy ones this year?" Each year he'll say the same thing, "About half-half." Incidentally, that's the ratio I found during my school days. How about you?

10. Award Bonuses, Prizes, Gifts, etc.

I've found that giving small bonuses, awards, and gifts to Stars and Steady Eddies helps to attract and retain them. But you have got to be careful. You don't want the bonuses to be too regular. People will expect them and the bonuses can demotivate them once they stop. Such awards become an addiction: the team isn't excited to get them but gets upset if they stop. Jim Collins says it best, "It's who you pay, not how you pay them."[26]

You also want to ensure they are achievable. If only 1% of the team gets the bonus, then 99% of the people will give up.

In Asia it's a good idea to have an individual bonus scheme and a team bonus scheme. Some people may even feel uncomfortable winning the individual award, but they will shout from the rooftops when their team wins the group award.

> **Tip:**
>
> If a winning team had a member (or more) who didn't achieve his or her individual target, then s/he was 'carried' by their team members. As a result, I would take that person's bonus away and divide it among those team members who achieved their individual targets. I don't believe in rewarding Slugs.

> **Tip:**
>
> At one employer, the employees sat in rows of ten people each. I created a weekly incentive based on rows. I called it 'Row Warriors.' The winning row that week would win a USD 50 gift voucher per member. The first week or two, it generated a lot of enthusiasm. But then one row had better synergy and won week after week. The other rows soon gave up.

---

26   Jim Collins, Good to Great: *Why Some Companies Make the Leap ...and Others Don't* (New York: HarperCollins, 2001), 49.

A better program that generated more enthusiasm involved a large, flatscreen TV as a prize. The TV was placed in the front of the office for all to see. Next to it was an empty, sealed box. It had one opening for a slot. Anyone who persuaded a customer to pay by credit card got one ticket from his or her supervisor to put in the slot. At the end of the month, the department head reached his hand into the box to call out the ticket with the lucky person's name on it. Those who were more persuasive with customers had a better chance of winning, but nearly everyone had at least one ticket in the box.

I like to pass out cash. If our department exceeded the monthly target, the Finance Department would allocate some extra money. I'd go to the bank and withdraw the bonus money. I'd put it in a plastic bag and walk around the department, usually late in the day on a Friday. I felt like Santa Claus. I'd have a colleague stand next to me with the name list of the Stars and Steady Eddies and the amount each deserved. It caused a big scene whenever I walked down the rows with the cash bag. The name list was a wonderful tool to recognize that month's top performers. I already knew whose names were on the list, but I'd play dumb when I came to a someone not on the list. I'd ask my colleague, "Hey, is Guru on the list?" He'd say, "No, Steve."

I could then act incredulous. "Guru, I thought for sure you had a good month last month. What happened? (listen to him say a few excuses). Well, I'm sure I'll see your name on next month's list. Manage your time well. Good luck."

It felt wonderful to publicly recognize and criticize — in a non-threatening way.

Another idea came from our CEO. He awarded business-class airfare for two anywhere in the world to each member of a four-person project team that had successfully navigated our company through a complex, company-wide, IT-system upgrade.

At another employer, I'll never forget the time I won the monthly 'Summit Award' as a young employee. It was awarded by senior management to the best employee that month. We had over 1,000 employees. It was a special award in addition to our monthly performance bonus. When I won it, the 'big bosses' came to my cubicle to shake my hand and applaud. They gave me a small, crystal mountain statue with my name and award month engraved. Plus $250. I was mentioned in the company's newsletter. I was given a reserved parking spot at the building's front entrance for one month. My parking spot's sign read, "Summit Award Winner." When you entered the main entrance, guess whose photo you saw? Did it feel great? Hell yeah! The award used a combination of triggers. If you didn't like the fancy recognition, well maybe you'd like the $250, or maybe the convenient parking spot, or maybe the crystal mountain statue? There was something for everyone. I still remember it 25 years later.

When I ask bosses at other organizations if they have a bonus scheme, most say, "No." When I ask, "Why?" They say, "No budget." To me these are lazy supervisors. How much budget do you need to take a Star or team to lunch? For drinks? For Starbucks? Come on. The problem isn't the budget.

11. Give Frequent and Sincere Verbal and Written Recognition

There is no excuse for not giving your team members verbal or written recognition. You should do this daily. It costs nothing. In the next chapter, you will how the powerful E.E.C.+ (Example, Effect, Continue) model helps you do this. Giving sincere, specific, positive feedback is a powerful tool that increases motivation in most people. Supervisors are ready to highlight mistakes, but we need to take more time each day to give positive feedback.

One tip is to contact their family member and alert them of your team member's top performance. When you see your team member the next day, s/he will likely be wearing a smile. And the next time that team member complains about you to his or her family, the family member can say, "No, your boss isn't that bad. He seems very nice." You don't want to lose your

Stars! If their families like you, hopefully that can contribute to the Star staying with you a little longer.

Written Recognition Story:

Many years ago, I entered my parents' bedroom and found my mom standing there. I noticed a birthday card displayed on my dad's dressing cabinet. He had just reached 60 years old. The card was from his father.

It read:

> *"Dear Terry,*
>
> *Happy birthday. I am proud of you.*
>
> *Love,*
>
> *Dad"*

I turned to my mom and asked why such a simple card was standing on his dressing cabinet. "Shouldn't it be thrown out?", I added.

She said, "That's the first birthday card your grandpa ever gave your dad."

My grandfather arrived in America in the 1920s as an immigrant from county Donegal, Ireland. He worked as a doctor, a general practitioner. Although he was a fantastic grandfather, he wasn't the best father. He was a very traditional father who spent most of his time on work and did not interact much with his three children. Fatherhood was a serious business, a formal affair. Incidentally, I've seen way too many fathers with that mindset here in Malaysia.

My father had spent his entire life trying to gain his parents' approval, especially his father's. My dad was a top student, he went to medical school, became a successful ophthalmologist, and president of the ophthalmology association in Washington state. He was a great husband and a great father to five children.

Yet his parents treated his successes as an everyday occurrence. Nothing was ever recognized, let alone celebrated. Until his 60th birthday, when he received that card.

My mom said, "Your dad cried after he read it."

To me the card's message looked very basic, but to my dad it was the culmination of six decades. He kept the card for the rest of his life. The card's simple message showed two important points that we should never ignore: pride and love. Don't wait to show pride and appreciation to your team members for their successes.

12. Give Credit and Take Blame

When I see politicians on TV, they are almost always giving good news about low unemployment, new tax cuts, or a new student loan forgiveness system. They claim credit as if these successes were achieved all by themselves.

I rarely see them announce bad news like, "I'm sorry to report that our nation's unemployment rate has hit a 50-year high. Oh, and by the way, the price of petrol will increase another 25 cents tomorrow. Good night my fellow citizens."

No way! They let assistants give bad news.

This was easily seen during the COVID-19 pandemic. Some world leaders acted like magicians. They disappeared when the virus was hitting its hardest, then reappeared when it improved. I understand the need to be popular, but I also understand the need to show courage. Some leaders show courage better than others.

It shows courage when you allow your team members to claim credit. For some of them, it may be a career highlight. As President Harry Truman said, "It's amazing what you can accomplish if you do not care who gets the credit."

Captain John Mitchell is an example of a team leader who shared credit. At age 29, he allowed his team to claim credit for a successful military mission during World War II. In 1943, Captain Mitchell, a U.S. air force squadron leader who was based on Guadalcanal in the South Pacific, received intelligence that a plane transporting Isoroku Yamamoto (the Japanese Admiral and the leader of the attack on Pearl Harbor) would be in the vicinity.

Mitchell led his team of 16 P-38 Lightnings to Bougainville Island in Papua New Guinea to intercept and shoot down Yamamoto's plane. Mitchell chose his four best pilots to be on the 'hit squad.' He and the rest of the squad would fly at a higher altitude to interfere with any incoming enemy planes. The hit squad was successful. Yamamoto's death was a huge blow to the Japanese, both tactically and emotionally.[27] How many young leaders do you know who would NOT nominate themselves to be on the hit squad and instead let others claim the glory?

Interestingly, after the kill, one of the pilots claimed the kill all for himself. Another pilot, Lt. Rex Barber, also claimed credit. It was known as the 'Credit Controversy.' The air force initially gave each pilot half a kill, but—decades later—after forensic analysis on Yamamoto's wrecked plane, historians now agree that Barber was the lone gunman.

On the flip side, be courageous and take the blame when something doesn't go right. Don't make excuses. Humans are visual creatures; your team is watching your behaviors—both good and bad. Many of them will emulate you. Instead of blaming others and making excuses, accept the blame (or your part of it) and offer solutions. Harry Truman also had a plaque on his desk which read, "The buck stops here!"

Blaming others is part of human nature. It has been around since Adam and Eve. In the Book of Genesis, God asks Adam why he ate the apple? What does he do? He blames Eve. When God asks Eve, she blames the snake. Had God asked the snake, I'm sure it would have said, "The devil made me do it."

We all naturally push blame away, but it takes real courage to accept it. Even welcome it. When things go wrong, the key isn't to pinpoint and appoint blame. The key is what do we have to put in place to prevent it from happening again?

---

27   Daniel Ford, "'Dead Reckoning' Review: Taking Aim at a Target of One," *Wall Street Journal,* June 5, 2020, https://www.wsj.com/articles/dead-reckoning-review-taking-aim-at-a-target-of-one-11591365904 (Accessed January 10, 2021).

"Success has many children; failure is an orphan."

13. Ask Them

We may think we know what motivates our team. But until you ask them you won't really know. Not everyone thinks like you. Not everyone is motivated by money and advancement. Not everyone wants to become a supervisor. Years ago, my boss, Doug Faber, asked me what motivated me.

I said, "To work overseas."

Doug laughed and told me that they didn't have any offices overseas. He felt uneasy as he didn't think he could get me what I wanted. Six months later, we bought a 20% interest in a Malaysian telecommunications company. Doug suggested that I help start up the new venture. That two-month assignment lasted eight years and I'm still living in Malaysia. I'm glad he asked. He changed my life. If you want to become a memorable boss, help your team members achieve their dreams.

14. Run Fun Internal Team Events

At one large department I ran, we had a theme day on the last day of each month. Beach day, English Premier League Football day, Hollywood day, or whatever. The management team would select three themes, then pass the themes to the teams to decide. We found that this was faster than giving the department carte blanche to decide. We would then choose a few people to be in charge of that theme day and we'd give them a small budget to decorate the office, buy some after-work snacks, and get small prizes for the best dressed team members.

The responsible team members worked late into the night, preparing the office for the special day. It worked well since the teams were involved in the theme selection. They were committed to it. On World Cup theme day, some folks came to the office with their faces painted. It was all fun and helped reduce work stress. These were cheap, silly events that I will remember my whole life.

At the end of each quarter, each supervisor was involved in organizing a big after work contest that would be held at the workplace. It could involve getting cheap foosball tables, children toys, and silly games. Since it's at the end of the month, it would also have a theme. We'd give prizes to the winners and have a catered dinner at the workplace. Lots of fun and it was inexpensive.

15. Run Fun External Team Events

As the collections department head in Malaysia, I was luckier than most. We were awarded a monthly incentive if we exceeded the company's financial targets. I would pass out half the money to the top 30% performers. The other half was saved for future department purposes: after work dinners, bowling, short vacations, gift vouchers, movie tickets, cheesecakes, and whatever.

When I worked as a head in HR, our department of 30 took a half-day off and chartered a bus to a water theme park. We all returned to Kuala Lumpur by 10:00 p.m. It was fun.

In my American jobs we also had fun external events. Each summer, our banking team of 15 would take our largest customer's key employees for a chartered halibut fishing trip to Homer, 6-hours south of Anchorage. The night before we'd bond over dinners cooked on the beach during the midnight sun. We'd rent hotel rooms for our customers, but my team slept in our own campers, motor homes, and tents on the beach to keep expenses low. Early the next morning, we'd all meet at the fishing boat and ride around Kachemak Bay, catching delicious halibut. We always went home with fond memories of this great event—and a bag of halibut filets.

In Seattle, our department's 90 employees would take a 2-hour dinner cruise on Lake Washington after work. We'd all be home by 10:00 p.m. During the cruise, our department head would make special announcements and give awards to the Stars.

16. You

No matter what motivational environment you try to build within your organization it will fail if you yourself don't lead by example. By "walking the talk" you inspire people and help build the right motivational environment. Motivated — or de-motivated — organizations and teams reflect their leaders, including YOU.

Tay Yow Hong, a senior manager of Malaysia's Hap Seng Credit, said it best in an interview I had with him:

> Transformational leaders inspire, motivate, and encourage their staff to surpass their own self-interest, to innovate, and create changes to achieve the very best for their organizations. People feel glad to be working for such leaders.

My Chapter's Key Points:

- Each team member has different needs. Although their age can affect how they think, I'm against labeling people Gen X, Y, Z and assuming that everyone in that Gen thinks alike.

- Spoil your top performers rotten. You need them to achieve your results. It's OK to have favorites as long as it's based fairly on performance.

- Quickly alert people when they underperform to show that you are watching. Diagnose if it's a 'will' or 'skill' problem. Give them attention, coaching, or training to close the gaps. If there is still no improvement, help them get off the bus.

- Develop your people's strengths to make them superstars: The Fiddler Crab principle. Don't try to make a cat into a dog. You're just wasting time and causing unnecessary stress.

- You can't motivate people; only they can do that. But you can build a motivational environment. I have given you many ideas.

Managing people isn't easy, but it is impactful because you change people's lives. It's so impactful that the next chapter is devoted solely to coaching.

COACHING

"A coach is someone who tells you what you don't want to hear, who has you see what you don't want to see, so you can be who you have always known you could be."
– Tom Landry, professional American football coach

Coaching is the single most important supervisory function that you can do. You won't win if you don't have a top performing team. And you need to be an effective coach to get a top performing team. Your people will demand it. They want to improve their skills and to future-proof their careers. Without coaching, it will take your team members much longer – and endure more stress — to achieve peak performance. My colleague, Adzhar Ibrahim notes that, "Your purpose should be to help people fly versus stomping on them to get results."

The coaching function is so important that this chapter is focused solely on it. When done incorrectly, your supervisory power will inflict lasting damage. So, you need to master this skill to use your supervisory power positively. Like Peter Parker's uncle tells him in the movie *Spiderman*, "With great power, comes great responsibility."

Anders Ericsson was a psychology professor at Florida State University. His life's study focused how certain people achieved top performance.

[He] argued that sustained practice was far more important than any innate advantages in determining who reaches the top in athletic, artistic and other fields.[28]

That practice, however, couldn't be mindless repetition. He called for 'deliberate practice,' preferably guided by an expert teacher, focused on identifying and correcting weaknesses and monitoring progress.

You can see this in young kids' performances. Those parents who are able to provide personal coaches and tutors, whether it be for badminton or math, will have kids who perform better than those without personal coaches and tutors.

As supervisors we also need to discuss with our people on their career and personal ambitions. And how we can help them achieve their dreams.

Although coaching may be our most important job function, we might be too busy attending meetings and putting out fires most of the time. And when we get to it, we often do it incorrectly. Dear reader, I'm sure you have received a poor or no coaching experience at some time in your life. I'm sure the experience was unforgettably painful. Let's stop this cycle from happening to others and make the world a better place to work.

My Coaching Values

These values are the O/S that underpins my coaching style and the House coaching model that I will soon introduce.

---

28   James R. Hagerty, "Professor Studied How Elite Performers Reach the Top," *Wall Street Journal*, June 25, 2020, https://www.wsj.com/articles/professor-studied-how-elite-performers-reach-the-top-11593090001 (Accessed January 4, 2021).

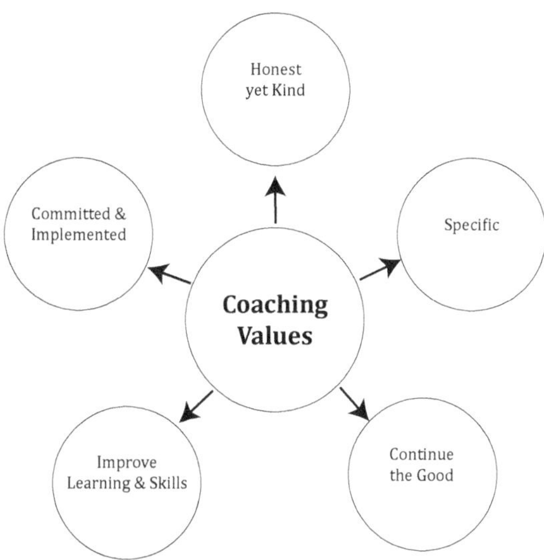

The House Coaching Model

The goal of this model is to end the coaching session with the employee feeling good and committed to a plan. It reinforces the positive values I mentioned earlier, while addressing the negative aspects.

The House Coaching Model has five steps and starts from the top:

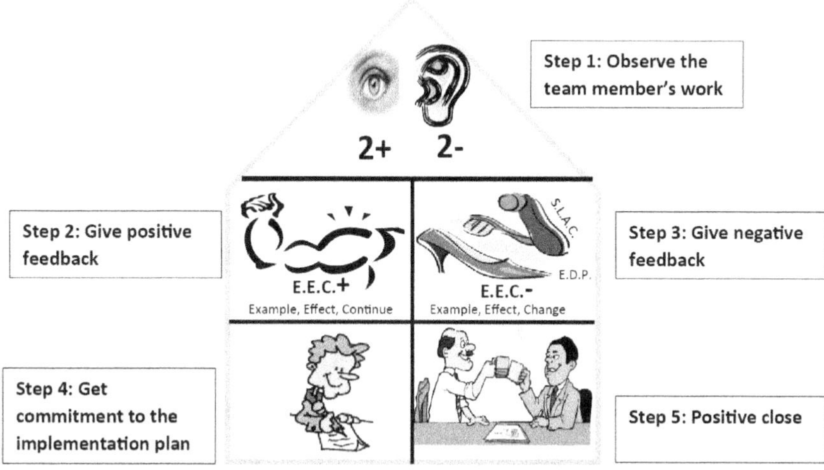

Step 1: Observe the Team Member's Work

You do this either visually or aurally. Either way, you start by observing one or two important positive and negative items about the team member's actions (or inactions). When I coach, I don't like to overwhelm people with too many positives or negatives. Giving too many positives makes it sound like you're piling on the bull-crap. Give too many negatives makes people become demotivated. It could also be seen as cruel. You can't make your team members perfect after one coaching session. Be patient. "Rome wasn't built in a day."

Ideally, you should write (or type) down what you liked and disliked. This way, you can quote or show the exact words and facts when you give the feedback. This makes the feedback harder for the employee to dispute. Use verifiable facts, not pure opinion. Key facts could include dates, time periods, numbers, words used, customer's name, project name, actions, etc. Facts make you sound prepared, confident, and fair. Unsubstantiated opinions have the opposite effect.

Here's an example of fact-based feedback: *"When I heard you talking to Mr. Chong, you said '...' And he said, '...'*

Example of opinion-based feedback: *"I can't remember the person's name. Maybe it was Mr. Ching. I think you said something to the effect of '...' And I think he said, '...'*

Step 2: Give Positive Feedback via EEC+ (The Strengths)

Look back over the course of your life. What were your happiest moments? I bet those moments involved something positive happening to you. Perhaps it was a new job promotion and compliment from your boss? Maybe it was the first girl who said "yes" when you summoned the courage to ask her for a date? Or a nice remark from a teacher for a job well done? Or a parent, spouse, or loved-one who told you that you are loved? Or the first hug from your child?

In my life, positive feedback has shaped me into the person I am today more than negative feedback has. Of course, negative feedback teaches a lot – and sometimes the lessons are painful--but my positive moments give me the strength to live and overcome the negative moments. The most powerful positive feedback came from others. From parents and family members telling me they loved me, to childhood friends who told me I was 'cool', to my baseball coach and team mates congratulating me for hitting a grand slam when I was 12-years old, to the first girl who told me I was 'cute', to my past bosses, team members, peers, and customers who told me they liked working with me.

As bosses we often highlight our team's negative behaviors and attitudes so that we can achieve the results, but this quest for negativity is dangerous as it excludes the search for positivity and the many benefits it brings. Between positive and negative feedback, positive feedback is the more important of the two, yet it's also the more neglected one.

Most people's primal purpose in life is to seek pleasure, bliss, happiness, serenity, service, self-actualization, or whatever you want to call it; and people like it when they receive properly delivered honest positive feedback because it's pleasurable. Hell, even receiving it improperly feels good!

Besides being pleasurable, positive feedback has other benefits:

- It builds communication, trust, and respect between the giver and the receiver which improves relationships, teamwork, and motivation.

- It promotes honesty.

- It allows the receiver to feel like a winner—and everyone likes to win.

- It helps your team members enjoy the coaching experience and not dread it.

- It allows the listener to be more open to you when you do have to highlight negative behaviors or attitudes that need changing.

Spend as much time giving positive feedback, if not more, than when giving negative feedback. Unfortunately, supervisors often take positive behaviors for granted. They shouldn't. There's a passage in the Bible, 1 Corinthians 12:31-13:13, "If I speak without love, I am no more than a gong booming or a cymbal clashing." We highlight positive behaviors and attitudes because we want our team to see that we value such behaviors and attitudes in them AND we want them continued.

Now let's talk about the mechanics of delivering feedback.

Conduct your feedback session in a private setting as giving and receiving feedback is sensitive. When you contact your team member for the meeting, make it look like you enjoy the coaching task. Don't treat it like a chore. Make some small talk before going into your positive and negative observations.

I give the positive feedback first. I don't care how tough the person receiving the feedback is, people like compliments. We are sensitive creatures with frail egos. You can either give the two positive observations first, then move to the two negatives. Or give one positive, one negative, one positive, and one negative. Your choice.

If your organization suffered financially during COVID, then giving positive feedback is especially important. When you are in an organization that is eliminating or reducing people's salaries or bonuses, it might be the only good thing you can impart as it's free.

When I share the positive behavior I observed, I use my EEC+ (Example, Effect, Continue) technique:

- Example is the specific example that you observed. It's the situation's 'what.'

- Effect is the 'why' of the event so that the employee sees the big picture.

- Continue shows that you want that positive action to continue back on-the-job. It shouldn't be a one-off occurrence.

Let's give your team member, Jessica, two positive feedback points using EEC+:

1. "Jessica, I attended two hours of your IT training for the Customer Service department today. I liked how you ensured that the test systems didn't crash during the training session **(EXAMPLE).** Your good preparation skills enabled the learners to get more hands-on experience and increased their confidence **(EFFECT).** Please keep it up **(CONTINUE).**"

2. "I also liked that you used Zack as your assistant **(EXAMPLE).** He was able to walk around the room and help the learners when they had system problems. It gave you more time to cover more subject areas **(EFFECT).** I suggest using him for your next training **(CONTINUE).**"

Often, bosses give us positive feedback like, "Good job, Steve." But we have no idea what job s/he is talking about. No examples. No 'what.'

Or maybe they'll say something like, "Steve, good job handling the Singapore account." Now you have the example, but you don't know the effect (the 'why').

Let's share another EEC+ example with an employee named Zainol:

"Zainol, good job handling the Xarax account in Singapore. They were upset with our service, but you calmed them down using active listening **(EXAMPLE).** And you saved us from losing their business worth RM100,000 annually **(EFFECT).** By the way, Ahmad, the head of sales here told me they just ordered another shipment worth RM20,000 **(more EFFECT).** Please keep up the good work **(CONTINUE).**"

EEC+ is sincere because you took the time to give detailed feedback.

Q: What if you can't do EEC+ as you didn't observe anything positive about what your team member did?

A: Don't immediately go into negativity mode. You've got to find something positive. It could be their intentions. They probably intended to do the action well. Or perhaps you can give them a compliment for trying? Or even bring up a past success. You must find something positive! Is it two-faced? Maybe. Still, humans are humans, and you can't just whack people with criticism. It's unkind and demoralizing. Like doctors, supervisors *"should do no harm."*

> **Tip:**
>
> You can also compliment the qualities it took to achieve the positive result. E.g., "I know it took good time management skills on your side to meet the deadline."

Step 3: Give Negative Feedback via EEC- (The Weaknesses)

HR departments call this 'improvement feedback' or 'constructive feedback, ' but whatever you call it, employees (especially young and thin-skinned individuals) can take it negatively. I call it EEC- (Example, Effect, Change). As a coach, you want to immediately extinguish negative behaviors and attitudes. If you don't address the negative issues quickly, they develop into habits that can spread like cancer. The key difference with EEC- is that you want the bad behavior to stop and change into something better.

Try not to be demoralizing when giving negative feedback. In the diagram for the House Coaching Model, you will see an illustration of a shoe brush. My goal is to help the team member polish his or her technique. No matter who we are, we can all polish up our work performance. Another way to think of it is as you are providing the missing ingredient they need to achieve more.

Let's look at two items that Jessica could have improved during her training session:

1. "Now I noticed that a young man asked you a question about the server. And an older man, with glasses, asked you a question about the system configurations. You couldn't answer both questions. This is fine because we don't know everything. It's just that you didn't provide them a workaround **(EXAMPLE)**. When you are unable to give an answer, I suggest you inform that person that you will research it during the lunch break. That way, you look confident and helpful. You, and the class, will also learn when you share the answers after lunch **(EFFECT).** In the future, please write down any questions you can't answer and share the answers with the group later, OK?" **(CHANGE).**

2. "I also noticed that when the system hung for a while you said, "Sorry everyone, such a stupid system" **(EXAMPLE).** I know you were frustrated, but when you attack the system that you are training, you lose credibility. You can also increase their job stress **(EFFECT).** As a fellow member of management, we must support our systems and processes to instill confidence in our teams. In the future, please don't express your negative opinions in public. Do that with me privately, OK?" **(CHANGE).**

When your team members receive your negative feedback, some will definitely dispute it. That's OK, negative feedback isn't easy to hear. The Chinese call feedback 'medicine for the ears.' I use a conflict resolution tool called SLAC: Stop, Listen, Assert, Cooperate. But let's return to that after I finish explaining my House Coaching Model.

Right now, let's look at my EDP (Explain-Demonstrate-Practice) model. Its main objective is to coach team members to change their negative behavior. EDP lies within the House model.

EDP (Explain-Demonstrate-Practice) Technique

Changing a negative or incorrect behavior is tough once it becomes a habit. When I coach, I often conduct mini-training sessions within the feedback session to teach and reinforce the new skill or habit. With complex skills, just telling people what to do is not enough — you need to show them. Then, make them show you to cement the change in their brains. Changing behaviors that hinder a person's performance helps them to unleash potential they never knew they had.

Let's say you've listened to a few sales calls by your new team member, Bob. He's having problems overcoming a prospect's price objections while selling your company's industrial air purifiers. When customers say, "It's too expensive," Bob responds with, "But our quality is better." Then he tries to close the sale. Unfortunately, customers don't believe his claim because he hasn't fully explained why the quality is better.

Let's imagine that you have already shared the one or two positive and negative observations via EEC+ and EEC- with him. Bob is aware that he has problems in handling price objections and he's not resistant to change. Now, as an experienced sales leader, you need to conduct a mini-training session to cement the new behavioral change using EDP.

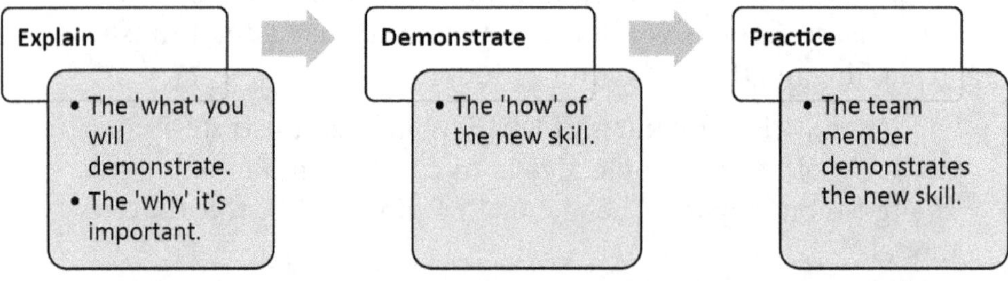

Explain: "Bob, when I sold this product, I also had the same issues you're having. Price objections are tough as our air purifiers cost 20% more than others. You need to overcome these objections as they're very common **(the 'what')**. When you do, you will have a greater chance of hitting your sales targets **(the 'why')**. I overcame price objections by mentioning that our air purifiers only need a filter change after 10,000 hours of usage; whereas our competitors' filters must be changed every 5,000 hours. And our filters can be easily replaced by the customer. They don't have to wait for our technician to change it and get charged for the service. So, customers enjoy our lower operating expenses. Plus, they're in control of the maintenance."

Demonstrate: "Bob, let's try that call again. This time I will be you and you will be the customer, Mr. Tan. Now, please give me the price objection. [Bob, throws a price objection].

> "You're correct, Mr. Tan. Our price is 20% higher. That's because our air purifiers' filters last an extra 5,000 hours versus our competitor's. Ours last 10,000 hours. That's 416 days before a filter change. We have the longest lasting air purifier filters on the market. And you can change the filter yourself. You don't have to wait for a vendor's technician to visit and charge you for it. Over the long term, you save more money and down time with our air purifiers than any others. What do you think?
>
> "So, how many air purifiers would you like me to ship today?"

Practice: "OK, Bob? Now you try. I'll be Mr. Tan and I'll throw the price objection. [You throw the objection and Bob practices the new skill. You may need to do this more than once until Bob feels confident with handling the price objection].

Doing mini-training sessions or EDPs shows your team member that you care about his or her success. It also alerts you to which team members can change and which ones can't. Not all people are cut out to do certain jobs. EDPs tell you which team members are worth spending your limited coaching and training time on. And which team members need to change seats or be escorted off the bus.

Not Giving Negative Feedback (or Giving It Late) Is Worse Than Giving It Early

When I was a new supervisor, I felt uncomfortable giving negative feedback to my team, especially to team members who were older than me. I wanted to be liked. Unfortunately, such behavior isn't fair to your team or your employer. You are basically lying because you aren't telling people the truth.

In my case, I was unfair to a team member because I didn't help him improve. I was unfair to my employer because they paid me to achieve results and solve problems, not ignore them. Instead, I was a lying coward. I delayed giving the slightly painful negative feedback until the year-end. My team member thus had an excruciating surprise during his year-end performance appraisal. Afterwards, he asked for a different supervisor. I didn't blame him.

I justified my cowardice by telling myself that I didn't want to hurt his feelings, but it was really all about my own gutlessness. In my first year as a supervisor, I was a nice but terrible boss. I hope your first year went better than mine.

What helped me regain my courage was the principle of fairness. In our work lives, fairness is more valuable than niceness.

Being a 'Teddy Bear' Is Worse Than Being an Honest, Fair Supervisor

When you give negative feedback, your team members will make all sorts of excuses. They may even give you solid reasons for their poor results. Excuses should be immediately (but kindly) rejected. You and your team have no time for excuses. Instead, focus on the results and the change that you want them to make to achieve those results.

If their reasons for failing are legitimate objections (e.g., poorly structured department systems and processes; roadblocks in other departments), you may be able to eliminate some of these reasons to make your team member's job smoother. Still, there are many limitations that we cannot change. We have to live with them. One technique I use when an employee gives solid reasons for their poor performance is to show that other team members have overcome the same hurdles.

It's better to be a fair and courageous lion than a friendly yet unfair teddy bear. Teams respect tough but fair bosses who achieve success. They won't respect friendly losers.

Step 4: Get Commitment to the Implementation Plan

Since you're taking valuable time to coach a team member, it's senseless to end the session without an implementation plan.

You want three items in the plan:

1. Summary of the plan.
2. Team member's agreement and commitment.
3. Timeline. When it will be enacted?

If you lack any of these three items, you've just wasted two people's time.

Let's return to Jessica:

1. Summary: "So, Jessica. You agree that you will continue to prepare the IT system well before each training session to reduce the chance of system crashes. And you will continue using Zack or another back up to assist you with any PC problems, right?"

"And, if you can't answer any of the learners' questions, you will get the answers later and share them with the learners like after lunch or another tea break, right? And you won't criticize the system, or any management decision in public, right?"

2. [Jessica gives her agreement and commitment]

3. Timeline: "So, when will you **commit** to this plan?"

[Jessica gives the timeline. Hopefully it's "today."]

> **✍Tip:**
>
> When gaining agreement, both the team member, and especially you, should avoid words like, "Try to...", "I hope you can...", and "Hopefully you will...." These are weak words that avoid a firm commitment. Ensure everyone uses decisive words. If Jessica says she will 'try,' respond with, "Thanks for trying, Jessica. But I really need you to do it, OK?"

Q: What do you do if you see Jessica saying, "Yes" to the commitment to change, but her body language and tone say, "No"?

A: *'Name the Game'.* Highlight what you observed. Working in an environment of uncertainty or subterfuge won't lead to the results you want. You need her commitment, otherwise this whole coaching session was for naught. *'Name the Game'* is merely getting to the truth.

E.g.

> "Jessica, when I asked for your commitment you said, 'Yes.' But you looked down and your tone didn't sound like you believed in what I was saying. What's going on?"

When you *'Name the Game'* do it in a non-threatening, calm tone. This is a quest for the truth. If she says something that you don't like, don't get angry. Be happy you are getting the truth. I'd much prefer an ugly truth than a beautiful lie.

You want Jessica to get out any frustrations or fears about you, the job, her doubts, whatever. Afterwards, you want her agreement to commit to the implementation plan. She is a paid employee of the company and you are a representative of the company's management. Bottom line: She needs to do as management requests—as do you—for the company to succeed.

Another nice effect of *'Naming the Game'* is your team will see that good and bad behavior is addressed, not ignored. Your good performers will like this as they'll get recognition for their good behaviors. Your bad performers won't like it, but who cares? At least they'll be 'on-their-toes.' You are showing your team that you welcome good behaviors and quickly address negative behaviors. It's especially useful for borderline team members who may underperform if they are not observed and coached. Or will underperform if they see you don't do anything when others underperform.

Humans are visual creatures and watch what you do—or don't do—and act accordingly.

Step 5: Positive Close

This is the easiest step. But in some respects, it may be the most important one. We need to end the coaching session on a positive, human note. Our goal is to preserve their self-esteem. Show confidence in the team member — even if your confidence in that person may not be that high. Don't leave them with doubts!

Examples showing your confidence in them:

- *"Well, I know next time I observe you; you'll be even better."*

- *"I enjoyed our chat. Good luck back on-the-job."*

- *"I have confidence in you to become a great performer. Thanks for your support."*

Push and Pull Techniques

In any coaching session, you can either 'push' the information to the team member or 'pull' it from him or her. The previous coaching examples used the 'push' style of feedback. The supervisor highlighted the positive and negative areas and what to continue and change. This technique works well if you are short of time and if you're coaching new, inexperienced employees. 'Pushing' is less effective with experienced team members.

'Pulling' is the opposite. It's getting most of the information from the team member. You give them more control during the coaching session.

Let's use the 5-Step House Coaching Model with the 'pull' technique:

Step 1: Observe the Team Member's Work: You just observed two team members, both technicians, speaking in the lunchroom. Thiru called Ravi an "idiot." You saw that Ravi was hurt. As Thiru's supervisor, you know he is one of your better team members. It took you by surprise that he said this. To maintain harmony within the team, you call Thiru in for some coaching.

But before 'pulling' information from Thiru about the incident, I suggest you push one or two EEC+'s his way to start the session on a positive note. For brevity's sake, I'm just sharing one EEC+ and one EEC-.

Step 2: EEC+: *"Thiru, congrats on last month's fault resolution report. I saw that you finished in second place out of our 20-person team* **(EXAMPLE)**. *I know it took hard work and expertise on your part and helped us achieve the company's target* **(EFFECT)**. *Nice job and please keep it up."* **(CONTINUE)**

"Now....

Step 3: EEC-: *"Today, in the lunchroom, I heard you call Ravi an 'idiot'.* **(EXAMPLE)** *Why?"*

('Pulling' the explanation from Thiru. Let's assume Thiru understands such behavior is wrong).

"Ravi is your junior. How do you think he felt and feels about you now?" ('Pulling' the **EFFECT**).

(Thiru explains the effect and shows remorse).

"What can we do to ensure this doesn't happen again to Ravi or any team member?" ('Pulling the **CHANGE**).

(Thiru gives a change solution, if acceptable, go to Step 4. If not, discuss more).

Step 4: Get Commitment to the Implementation Plan: *"So, do I have your commitment that you will continue to be one of our top technicians and avoid using negative words on our team members? And you'll apologize to Ravi?"*

(Thiru gives his sincere agreement and commitment)

"Starting when?"

(Thiru says, "Now.")

Step 5: Positive Close: *"Great. Thanks for the chat. Let's put this behind us. We've got a great team and both you and Ravi are key players."*

> ☞ **Tip:**
>
> A nice way to 'pull' feedback from team members is the question, *"What could you have done differently."* This positive question looks at both the good and bad aspects of what you observed.

Handling Conflict with SLAC (Stop-Listen-Assert-Cooperate)

Conflict will break out when you give negative feedback (EEC-). Humans, especially poor performers, can over value their skills. They "don't know what they don't know." Whereas top performers think everyone works just like them, so they undervalue their skills. They "don't know what they do know." This is called the Dunning-Kruger effect. Organizations are full of confident poor performers and not-so-confident good performers.

When it comes to conflict, I usually find myself arguing more with the poor performers.

I was an ESL (English as a Second Language) teacher in Poland for two years. My first year was in a secondary school, the second at a college. On my last day of teaching, had you asked me, "What kind of grade would you give yourself as a teacher?"

I would have responded, "B to a B+." And I might have argued with you if you told me I was a bad teacher.

Then I attended an intensive, month-long teacher training course. The course gave me knowledge and skills to be a better ESL teacher. Now, after that training, if you had asked me to grade myself as a teacher, I'd have given myself a C- to a C.

In Asia, most people dislike conflict and want harmony to reign, even if it's false harmony. In Malaysia, people avoid saying, "No." Instead they will say, "maybe", "cannot", or "possibly." If they are standing right in front of you, they will keep quiet and just smile rather than say, "No." That's what my wife did when I asked her if she wanted a second child.

But I'm American.

I've spent years calling and visiting people to pay their overdue debts. I LOVE conflict. Conflict shows honesty. Conflict shows caring. Conflict saves time as you get to their honest feelings quicker. I dislike those who lie and say everything is OK when there is hidden turmoil in their heart and mind.

So, when I encounter conflict, I welcome it with open arms instead of running away or fighting it. I want to understand it because once I understand it, I have a better chance of ending it. But to do that, you first have to focus on the other person and not yourself. That's a tough habit to start.

Stop	• When people argue or debate with you, the first thing you need to do is stop talking. If you want to change the word "Stop" to "Shut Up", I'm OK with that. It's hard to stop talking when you're in an argument, but you must.
Listen	• You've got to REALLY listen to the other party. Not pretending to listen while waiting (and reloading) to fire back. Say a few words like: "OK", "I see", "Alright", etc. • When the other party is done, show active listening by repeating their complaint or argument—even if you disagree with it.
Assert	• Assert your point of view. Since you showed active listening, you now have a better chance that s/he will now listen to you. I suggest your assertion be mostly factual and without too much emotion, although some emotion can work well (especially if the other person is emotional).
Cooperate	• By now, hopefully, the other party's brain is more rational and ready to move into a problem-solving mode. You may want to 'pull' the implementation plan from them and say, "So, what do you suggest are the next steps?" If their implementation plan is acceptable, go for it. If not, assert why you need something more.

Will this work 100% of the time? No! Not every supervisor-employee conflict ends with sunshine, unicorns, and the sound of trumpets.

Will your team member consider you fair? Probably. You listened to his or her side. You repeated their issues. You tried to cooperate with them. Does everyone need to like you? NO! We've already talked about this. We just need them to do their work to achieve the desired results.

SLAC Quick Reference Guide

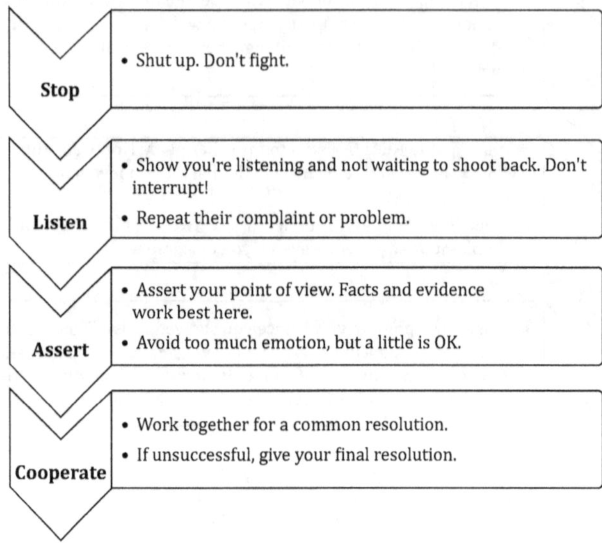

Termination Phrases to End a Coaching Session if No Agreement

Sometimes, no matter how hard we try, we are unable to come to an agreement with our team member. We just go round in circles. Now it's time to terminate the discussion and move forward. At this point, you might have to use the influencing factor: legitimizing (aka 'appeal to authority').

☝ **Tip:**

In explaining your decision, share the decision's 'what' and 'why.'

Here are some termination phrases:

- *"Well, it looks like we'll have to agree to disagree. In the meantime, we will.... (give your decision- the 'what') because.... (give your reason- the 'why')."*

- *"You have a right to your opinion; however, we will.... because...."*

- *"You are entitled to your point of view, as am I. So, we will.... because...."*

- *"I respect how you feel about that; however, we will.... because...."*

- *"I appreciate you had the courage to share your disagreement with me on this; however, I've decided that we will.... because...."*

- *"I respect your opinion and passion about this subject; however, as supervisor I have decided we will.... because...."*

> ☝ **Tip:**
>
> Don't use termination phrases on your boss, senior management, or the Board. Unless you want to be terminated yourself! For peers, you decide. But you may want to involve your boss to mediate those conflicts. For more ideas on handling difficult conversations, see the AUSE model in the next chapter.

Final Coaching Tips

Giving feedback takes finesse and the wrong word ruins everything.

Tips:

- Ask about the 'Why'? of a negative behavior allows the team member to explain why they did or didn't do something. It makes people feel like you first want to understand before passing judgment. It also avoids you jumping to conclusions, e.g. *"Why did you criticize your top-performing team member publicly?"*

- Ask about the 'How'? of the implementation plan (Step 4) involves the team member. E.g., *"How can we start getting to know our team members better?"*

- Avoid dangerous words like "always", "never", and "only." E.g., *"You never praise your employees."*

- Avoid timid words like: "try", "hopefully", and "I think." E.g., *"Hopefully you won't speak timidly to your team members."*

- Beware of 'If' as it can be viewed as a threat: *"If you don't start doing some of these new supervisory habits, you will be...."*

- Beware of 'should' as you sound like mom or dad: *"You should know by now that to be a good supervisor you need to...."*

- Beware of asking your team's feedback about you. I have made this mistake numerous times. It rarely succeeds in getting honest results. Your supervisor or HR personnel are better parties to ask for this information.

- Beware of the word 'but' when moving from the positive feedback (EEC+) to the negative (EEC-). Here are some 'but' alternatives:

  - "Now, there are two other areas that could be improved. First..."

  - "Now, there are two other matters that I'd like to highlight. First..."

  - "It's just that you need to start..."

- Welcome feedback on yourself, even if it's given to you poorly. No one is perfect. Ask for it frequently ask from your peers and superiors to maintain a strong organizational network.

  > *"If one person says that you are horse, smile at them.*
  >
  > *If two people say that you are a horse, give it some thought.*
  >
  > *If three people say that you are a horse, go out and buy a saddle."*

This Chapter's Key Points:

- Coaching is the most valuable contribution that you can make for your team members. Coaching promotes learning and growth. Coaching shows caring. Your team will remember how good (or bad) you coach them forever.

- The principles that drive my House Coaching Model:

    1. Get specific details you observed.

    2. Honest yet kind.

    3. Continue the good practices.

    4. Improve learning and skills.

    5. Secure commitment to the implementation plan.

- The House Coaching Model is a formal 5-step process to safely provide feedback to develop people and improve performance.

    Step 1: Observe one or two positive and negative actions. Focus on the most important ones.

    Step 2: Give positive feedback using EEC+ = Example, Effect, Continue. Positive feedback is a powerful tool in your toolbox. Give it frequently.

    Step 3: Give negative feedback using EEC- = Example, Effect, Change.

    - Use EDP = Explain, Demonstrate, Practice to cement any new skills you want your team member to display.

    - Use SLAC = Stop, Listen, Assert, Cooperate if you encounter conflict from your team member over your feedback.

Step 4: Get the team member's commitment and implementation plan to continue the good and change the bad behaviors.

Step 5: End on a positive note by expressing confidence in the team member and preserving all parties' self-esteem. This could be the most important step.

- 'Push' or 'pull' when giving feedback. 'Pushing' is when you are in control and tell the facts. 'Pulling' is asking the team member his or her reasoning on what you observed. 'Pushing' works well on new, younger team members. 'Pulling' works better on more experienced and senior team members.

The next chapter will focus on handling problems that you will encounter as a boss.

If you would like a free coaching checklist form to help you prepare for your next coaching session, just email me at: steve@servicewinners.com.

HANDLING PROBLEMS

No problems = No job.
— Steve Coyle

A boss's job is tough because people generally don't like being told what to do. A boss's workday won't be always smooth sailing. This chapter focuses on how to handle the choppy post-COVID waters you will encounter.

Making Decisions

How you solve problems—and how quickly you solve them—determines the amount of respect your team and others will have for you. Solving problems involves making decisions and sometimes the best decision is to do nothing. And at other times the best decision will be unpopular.

Lower and middle management employees make countless, daily operational decisions. Senior management employees make impactful decisions that affect the whole organization. Although senior management makes fewer daily decisions, I find the number one problem with them is the fear of making decisions. They have worked and networked so hard to reach that senior position that they become fearful of losing it. As we explained in Chapter 1, good leadership is about possessing courage and ethics. I don't consider leaders that lack either of these two qualities to be good leaders.

When making a decision, you need to balance the positives and negatives of that decision. No decision will be perfect, but the failure to decide is an abdication of responsibility. Of course, not all your decisions will be good ones, but as the author Herman Melville noted, "He who has never failed somewhere: that man cannot be great. Failure is the true test of greatness."[29]

Before making a decision, I first gather as much data, information, facts, inputs, and others' viewpoints as possible within the available time. In Chapter 2 we saw the value of having a diverse team to problem-solve diverse, complex problems. Diversity gives you more perspectives.

I was watching a BBC News story about an archeologist uncovering the ancient Roman city of Baiae[30] that is now underwater. I was amazed at how diverse his team was. The archeological team consisted of men and women from diverse nationalities, ethnicities, and skill sets. Although the chief archeologist was the 'boss', he acted more like an orchestra conductor.

His team composed of the following jobs and skill sets:

- Engineers to pilot underwater drones.

- Computer scientists to digitalize the ancient city's road maps, especially to digitalize the city's beautiful mosaics.

- Scuba divers to explore the area.

- Photographers to record the discoveries.

- Boat crew and captain.

- Oceanographers to map out the oceanic location.

- Biologists to determine which artifacts can survive the undersea microorganisms and which ones can't.

29   Herman Melville, quoted in "#Monday Motivation," Small Business, December 11, 2017, https://smallbusiness.com/monday-morning-motivation/failure-is-the-true-test-of-greatness/ (Accessed December 23, 2020).
30   "Italy's Sunken City", *BBC News*, https://www.bbc.co.uk/programmes/m000qsln (Accessed January 1, 2021).

- Volcanologist to determine if the volcanic vents shooting plumes of sulfuric acid near the ruins were hazardous.
- Cook to feed everybody.

In today's post-COVID work environment, we decision-makers face challenges that we have never faced before in our lifetimes. To increase our chances for making better decisions, we need a diverse team offering diverse brains.

Two-Lenses Decision-Making tool

Before making a decision, I want to gather as much information and inputs from as many sources as I can within the time-frame I'm allowed. Once I've done that, I'm ready to use a Two-Lenses Decision-Making tool.

1st Lens: What is the Overall Benefit of the Decision?
How will this decision affect my organization? E.g., team, department, boss, senior management, investors, stakeholders, customers. This first lens uses the utilitarian philosophy of maximizing the good for the maximum number of people.

2nd Lens: Can I Explain and Defend My Decision Well?
Can you legally, logically, and ethically explain and defend your rationale for making that decision at that time? If you can, then you have done your best under those circumstances. With hindsight, it may have even been the wrong decision, but it was the best decision at that time.

The Indecisive Boss Story 

Indecisive bosses lose their teams' confidence. At one of my ex-employers, I met up with one of my former Stars, Shashi, for drinks. He told me a frustrating story about his new boss, my replacement. Shashi, on his own initiative, collated a list of several thousand inactive customer accounts with small balances. Each account owed under RM40 (USD10). Although the accounts had been inactive for years, the company's IT system still managed them and sent out monthly print or e-bills. This cost the company more than what was owed. Shashi wanted to save the company money, reduce complaints, and clean up the IT billing system. He generated a 100-page report listing all such small accounts. Their total value was RM2,000 (USD 500). He asked his new boss to sign the approval to 'zeroize' that small amount and terminate thousands of inactive accounts.

The boss said, "Get my boss to sign it."

Shashi said that after seeing his boss's cowardice to make such a minor decision, he decided to resign. Employees judge their organizations by their bosses' actions and inactions. Although the company was a great company, he didn't see a future working with such a boss. Bad bosses who can't decide are insufferable. Besides being bad, they are also cowards. Could you work for such a role model? Bad bosses cause Stars to leave. Such bosses are 'empty vessels' occupying the boss's chair.

Michael Kinneman, VP of Financial Care for T-Mobile USA (and my ex-boss), said, "Surround yourself with people smarter than you. You don't have to be the brightest, but you should be the best decision-maker in the room."

Examples of Operational Problems

You will encounter countless operational problems at work and this book cannot cover them all. Let me cover a few examples and share how other bosses, including me, solved them. Hopefully, the examples will trigger ideas for you to solve your team's and organization's unique problems.

Sick Leave Problem

My department, generally, had strong teams. If everyone came to work, we could usually hit the company's financial target and receive a large monthly bonus. But everyone had to come to work. Unfortunately, our department suffered from a sick leave problem. Depending on which country you live, the labor law will state the maximum number of sick days one can be away. In Malaysia, sick leave is extremely generous. There is also emergency leave.

Our average team member was on sick or emergency leave 23 days a year. So, on average, each person missed one working month a year, not including annual leave. By contrast, my supervisory team and I, on average, missed about one day a year. The excessive sick leave affected our departmental results.

I tried to resolve this problem by having meetings with them. I'd explain how their sick leave affected the department's results. I had them run a committee among themselves to solve this sick leave issue. All these actions failed to solve the problem.

But once I changed the department's systems and processes, it worked.

First, I discovered the root cause of the sick leave problem was quite complex. When I joined the department, the operational processes allowed all team members to work overtime, even the poor performers. So staff would be sick one day, then work overtime the next day to recover their earlier lost statistics. Plus, they'd got paid overtime. It was a sweet deal. It paid being sick.

I changed the system and process by putting three new rules in place:

> Rule 1: Anyone on sick leave more than one day a month wasn't allowed to work overtime that month. They complained that I was punishing them for being sick. I responded, "No, if you're sick more than one day a month, I don't want you pushing yourself or you'll get sicker."

> Rule 2: Anyone who missed the department's average individual target the previous month couldn't work overtime the next month. I didn't want to pay poor or sub-par performers overtime. Slugs couldn't claim over-

time.

Rule 3: Anyone who worked overtime couldn't use those statistics in their monthly performance total. I discovered that the previous system punished those team members who couldn't work overtime due to family or other commitments. It wasn't fair.

Of course, there was resistance to the changes. But the average number of sick days per person per year reduced from 23 to 12. Still high, but at least we had a better chance of achieving our results. And we did. Our department won more awards due to its increased performance.

Nordea Insurance's Budgetary Problem in Poland

During one inordinately hot Polish summer, employees of Nordea Insurance requested that the company install air conditioners in their building. Unfortunately, this solution was impossible because of budgetary constraints. Their CEO, Pawel Miller, led the management and employee brainstorming session to create some workaround solutions.

Pawel told me that they decided that although there wasn't budget for a complete air conditioning system remodel, there was enough budget to purchase standing fans. The company's dress code was also relaxed for the summer months. Pawel also passed out free ice cream every day to the staff. Some days he even wore a white ice cream seller's hat. The employees would joke, 'Hey boss, I want strawberry tomorrow.'

Pawel shared these practical lessons when encountering operational issues:

1. Acknowledge the team's pain.

2. Share in the pain. The executive office was at the top floor (the hottest floor), but they also didn't receive air conditioning.

3. Involve the team in problem-solving.

4. Be flexible.

5. Poke fun at the pain.

Prayer Time problem

At my former Malaysian employer, we had approximately 50 Muslim team members. Muslims need to pray five times per day; two of those times are during the standard 9:00-5:30 pm workday. To pray, they had to take a lift down several floors to the dark carpark basement. Then back. Although the prayer process lasted only 5-10 minutes, the trip down and back, plus any distractions along the way caused more time wastage. Some of the female team members also felt uncomfortable going to the basement.

My Muslim team members asked if they could convert an unused storage space in our office to a *surau* (prayer hall). Great idea. I approved it. After they converted the area, the time savings were immediately felt. Productivity increased. Senior management was happy with our results, but the Facilities department was unhappy as I had used office space for another purpose. Luckily their head, the CFO, was happy with our increased financial performance and he ensured that his Facilities people wouldn't give us any problems. The overall benefit justified the cost for that decision as we hit our targets and made our Muslim staff happy.

Normal operational problems boil down to three main causes:

1. Miscommunication or failure to act.

2. Poorly designed systems and processes.

3. Lack of proper resources.

It takes time to get at the root of the problem. But once you get your facts and discover the root causes, you can generate a strategy to solve them.

Team Members' Complaints About Each Other

It's normal when you have people working together for hours at a time — in confined spaces — to have tempers flare. When dealing with minor human conflicts, I generally ask the parties to first resolve it themselves. They can do this at work or outside it.

If they still can't resolve it, then I get involved. I tell them that I'm disappointed that they cannot resolve it themselves. I now become a judge. I hear both sides. I then 'tai chi' the problem back to them as I'd much prefer that the solution came from them. If they still don't or can't offer a solution (or it's a poor solution), then I give the solution that works best — first for the team, then second for them.

The Jackie Story

One of my team members (a 'Slug') complained to me about our department's Superstar: Jackie.

Jackie was the youngest person in my department. She was also very attractive. She would come to her Malaysian workplace in a short skirt. It wasn't a mini skirt, but it was short. From my experience, I find that it's usually other women (and not the men) who complain when a woman wears sexy clothes to work. Our department was mostly Muslim, and Nori, a young Muslim female, complained that Jackie's short skirts were distracting the men.

I didn't see any deterioration in our results due to Jackie's short skirt.

How would you have handled Nori's complaint? Would you tell your best Star to dress more conservatively? Remember, I'm a middle-aged man and Jackie is half my age. She's also a Star whom I don't want to demotivate.

I explained to Nori that I didn't see any harm in Jackie's short skirts. Nori then tried another tactic: she said it violated HR's dress code. Again, I didn't see any violation. Nori still insisted that I talk to Jackie and tell her to dress more conservatively.

Jackie has helped me achieve many departmental bonuses. She makes me look like a hero to senior management. She comes to work on time, is always motivated, and nearly always wears a smile.

On the other hand, Nori is a below average performer. She has worked in the department for years and her performance rarely rises above average. I think you already know what I decided. I'm not going to risk demotivating my Star because a Slug wants me to tell her how to dress. Also, Jackie's job is over the phone and customers will never see her.

I gave Nori my decision: "Get your results up to Jackie's level, then come talk to me."

Complaints About Racism, Sexism, and Sexual Harassment

Definitely investigate immediately if there is a complaint about racism, sexism, sexual harassment, or other serious negative behaviors. No matter if the employee is a Star or a Slug. These are major issues that must be investigated. At one of my American employers, there would be an investigation if someone was called a racist. If the allegation was true, that person would undergo training. If the training was unsuccessful, s/he would be fired.

At the same employer, if someone was accused of sexual harassment or watching pornography at work, there would also be an investigation. If found guilty, that person was fired immediately. As a supervisor, you need to protect your team members, your company, and yourself. If you get these serious accusations, you need to act immediately. Involve HR in such serious issues to protect yourself and all parties. Follow the laws in your jurisdiction.

Family Complaints

I don't like to get involved in these kinds of complaints. Instead, I recommend that the team member sort it out with his or her family.

At one American employer, we had a married Star who was bisexual. He had a picture of his wife and his boyfriend at his desk. The boyfriend, a fellow employee, was HIV positive and near death — but he continued to work. This was during the 1990s, before an effective AIDS treatment existed.

The employee's wife called our department head insisting that he break up the men's relationship. She feared contracting AIDS from her husband. It was a complicated case, but the management decided to not get involved in the sexual relations between adults. My boss advised the employee to work it out with his wife. They eventually divorced.

Team Members' Personal Problems

In Western organizations, many employees feel comfortable sharing their personal problems with their supervisors. This is rare in Asia. In Asia, supervisors need to probe (politely and softly) to get their team members to share their problems. Otherwise, the employees internalize the problems, and you won't discover them until too late — when they resign or fail to come to work.

Two Cases of Personal Problem in an Asian Context

> Story 1: Roxy was a young top performer. Outside of work, she had a nasty romantic breakup with an older man. The man then became a stalker and Roxy's mental stability was shaken. She couldn't focus on work. Her parents hired a private detective to protect her. She, her parents, and the private detective met with me to ask for a six-month unpaid leave of absence. Since she was one of my Stars, I agreed. But after six months passed, she still didn't return to the workplace. She was terminated.

It was unfortunate, but I don't regret granting the leave of absence for a Star performer.

Story 2: Azri was involved in a serious car crash. He was a Steady Eddie. He asked for a 3-month leave of absence. I granted it. After three months he returned to work. I thought he would become a better, more committed employee, but he returned to his pre-accident Steady Eddie performance level. I regretted granting him the leave as I could have replaced him with someone who likely would be at least an 'average' or maybe even a Star. I'd rather take my chances on someone I don't know, than on a Steady Eddie that I do know.

I've spent years in the field of debt collections, and I've found that the best predictor of debtors' future payment behavior is their past payment behavior. I try to use the same rule with my team. When I get a special request from an employee that incurs a sacrifice from the team, I look at his or her past performance. If it's good, I'll likely grant it. If it's bad (to me: average is bad), I don't. Why would I significantly help that person if that person hasn't significantly helped the team?

You are evaluated by customers, senior management, the Board, and investors on the results you achieve or don't achieve. I will do whatever I ethically can to achieve those results while building a motivational work environment. I'm an ethical and courageous supervisor who can make tough decisions.

Team Members' Complaints About Their Boss

Complaints from the staff about their immediate supervisor are common. Who likes bosses? In one position, I was a manager who supervised several supervisors. When I got complaints from their team members about them, I went through a process:

> Step 1: I ask for details about the staff's complaint. I then ask if the supervisor was 'fair.' If s/he was fair, then I advise the staff (and sometimes the supervisor) to get along and get back to work as we have a responsibility to perform in our jobs. A lot of conflict between people isn't because someone is unfair, but because there was a miscommunication. As emotional beings, our brains 'jump' when we hear certain things and we rush to judge people negatively when really, they simply miscommunicated.

> If I determine the supervisor's behavior was unfair, then I'll take it to Step 2.

> Step 2: I'll ask for the supervisor's side of the event to get more details. I ask him or her if that was the best way to handle it. Normally the supervisor will share some suggestions for improvement. That's OK. We're all learning.

> Step 3: I'll ask the supervisor to meet with the staff to iron out any difficulties. Open communication reduces most conflicts.

Sometimes I get a complaint from one of my own team members about me. The earlier SLAC model works well. When people complain about you, it's only natural to get defensive. But you need to **Stop** and **Listen** to their complaint — justified or unjustified. Then **Assert** your side of the issue. Then **Cooperate** on a resolution. Normally, just the simple act of Stop and Listen is enough for your team member to get the issue out in the open. It can relieve their stress and sometimes resolve the issue. Apologies also work well here.

As a supervisor, don't punish staff for communicating their conflict – as long as it's done politely. It's much better to encourage your team to express conflict openly than to keep it buried inside and fester.

Complaints About Working Remotely

Some of these complaints can't be solved as the work environment has changed, but you can show your team members listening, understanding, and empathy. And sometimes that's enough. The AUSE model (explained later in this chapter) will help you.

Your job's focus will likely change from a people-management focus to a process-improvement focus. Your role will become more backend. You will spend more time removing your team's roadblocks like IT, HR, home office, even personal problems like daycare issues! Your goal is to allow them to work uninterruptedly and with the freedom to do it as they see fit (provided they achieve the results). In a sense, you are an IT manager, HR manager, operational manager, and counselor all rolled into one. The key question you need to ask your remote people is, "How can I help you achieve more?"

Remote work likely will lead to more employee burnout. In the office they could chat with a friend at lunch or in the pantry to relieve their stress, but at home they are constantly surrounded by their work and home pressures.

As Robert Sutton observes in the *Wall Street Journal:*

> A study conducted by one 350-person team at Microsoft Corp. found that in the four months after the team moved to remote work in March (2020), employees worked an average of four more hours a week, attended more (albeit shorter) meetings, and spent about 10% more time in meetings. Fragmented 'Swiss cheese' days

became common as people struggled to care for and teach their children, and to meet other personal obligations. A 'night-shift' emerged: Employees sent 52% more instant messages between 6 p.m. and midnight. They worked more hours on weekends. [31]

Your team may feel dislocated from the office and infer negative meanings from communications coming for HQ and you. They may also be 'always on' 24 x 7 by continuously checking their emails and IMs. For some Stars, you may have to force them to disconnect from work to reduce the chance for burnout. One idea is for teams to have "airplane mode afternoon". [32] The frequency and duration are up to you, but team members should turn off their WIFI and work uninterruptedly on important business — even personal tasks.

Customer Complaints: The AUSE Technique (Acknowledge, Understand, Solve, Empathize)

The AUSE technique is useful if you deal with external or internal customer complaints. These complaints—either written or verbal—are generated when people are angry. Your goal is to calm the angry person, protect your team and organization, preserve the relationship, and solve the problem(s). The expression "anger follows hurt" is true. And part of the process of calming angry people involves digging to unearth the other person's hurt.

Some complaints are justified, others unjustified. Some complaints are rational and calm, others are irrational and angry, and some are a mixture of both. All have hurt buried within the complaint — otherwise they wouldn't be contacting you.

---

31   Robert I. Sutton, "Remote Work Is Here to Stay. Bosses Better Adjust," *Wall Street Journal*, August 2, 2020, https://www.wsj.com/articles/remote-work-is-here-to-stay-bosses-better-adjust-11596395367 (Accessed August 30, 2020).

32   Ibid. Sutton borrows this concept from Kürsat Özenç and Margaret Hagan's *Rituals for Work: 50 Ways to Create Engagement, Shared Purpose, and a Culture that Can Adapt to Change* (New York: Wiley, 2011).

I've created the dual-purpose AUSE model that:

1. Calms angry people, and

2. Solves problems

When people are upset, they have two needs:

1. To be understood **How** (feelings) they feel and **What** (facts) the problem is. Their feelings are often more important than the solution.

2. To get a solution and stop the pain.

Responding to written customer complaints is easier than handling face-to-face or phone-to-phone complaints. While the AUSE model works for written, phone, and face-to-face complaints; it works best verbally.

Alaskan story

Handling angry people remind me of dealing with Alaska's cloudy glacial rivers. If you scoop up some of the water and immediately try to drink it, your mouth gets a dose of 'rock flour' (crushed rock dust from the glacier upstream). But, if you give the water **time**, the rock flour settles, and you can enjoy an ice-cold, pristine drink.

What are these shapes?

Circles?

Most people's brains will rush to complete the dashes and turn them into circles. But they're really just circular patterns.

Our brains like to 'jump' and solve problems quickly — but jumping tends to make angry people angrier. We need to take the time to show others that we understand their issues. They want you to first acknowledge and understand what they have gone through before they want your solution.

I've created this visual diagram to make it easier to remember. It reminds me of an eye chart. It has three simple steps, plus empathy. The key word I use to show empathy is, "Sorry."

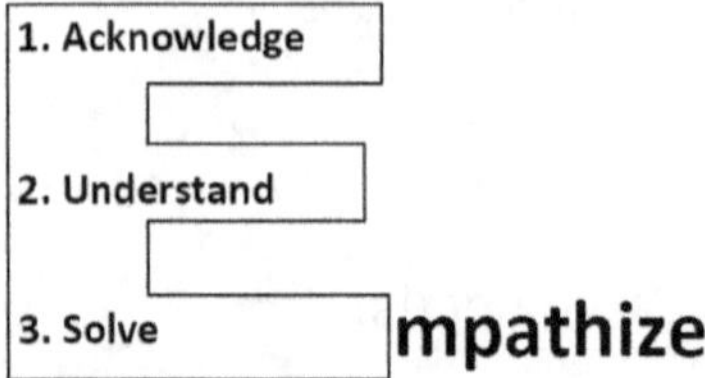

mpathize

Step 1: A = Acknowledge

As supervisors, we are under time constraints. We like fast solutions, but don't rush angry customers with your solutions. You need time to get them on your side first.

Verbally you show upset customers that you are listening by acknowledging them. These are small words that show that you are alive and breathing. If you're face-to-face, you do this by nodding and other gestures.

Some spoken examples:

- *"Oh my!"*
- *"I see."*
- *"Is that right?"*
- *"I can't believe that happened to you."*
- *"I would feel the same."*
- *"That's terrible."*
- *"Alamak!"*

When people are upset, they have an internal story inside their head that needs to come out. If you want to preserve the relationship, and save time, you have got to listen to the story. Don't interrupt and jump to the solution! At this stage, the angry person is in control of the conversation, not you. This stage takes a long time because angry people like to repeat themselves.

When people are hurt, you need to give them time—like rock flour—to let the pain settle. Until then, you can't get an irrational person's brain into a rational, problem-solving mode. Time is the best solution that I know of to make an irrational, angry brain become a calm, rational brain. Sometimes, if the pain is too deep and the solution isn't needed immediately, I'll ask the other person if we should speak at another time when they feel less pain.

People raise their voices when they feel that you are not listening. Careful acknowledgment shows listening and caring. And I'm not talking about the people who say, "yes, yes, yes" and seem to not really listen and just want you to finish so that they can speak. This isn't listening; it's waiting. It's waiting for their turn to speak.

Sometimes angry people call you names like "stupid", "idiot", or worse. Instead of disagreeing or fighting with them, I agree. "Yes, sometimes I may be an idiot. And I'm sorry about that." [Note: I wouldn't do this in a written response!]

What's the effect when you agree with him or her about what they call you?

Shock.

When people are in shock, this is the perfect time to take control. It takes courage to agree when they call you something negative. Let people win stupid name calling arguments if you can win when it comes to the solution. Lose the silly battles, win the war.

Once they're done venting, quickly move to the next step: Understand.

Step 2: U = Understand (and Confirm)

This step may be the most important step. Because if you don't do it well, your customer's anger will re-ignite. To show understanding, you need to repeat and confirm his or her concern.

In telephone conversations, I usually say, *"Let me see if I understand you,* (I then repeat the angry person's feelings and facts), *correct?"*

E.g., *"John, let me see if I understand you. You're angry*

because one of my staff promised she would solve this matter last Friday and as of today, Tuesday, it's still not solved. And she didn't call you to give you the reason for the delay. Is that correct?"

If I'm speaking with someone face-to-face, I'll repeat their concerns in a less formal way.

> 👆 **Tip:**
>
> Most supervisors repeat or summarize the issue's facts, but they forget to repeat the speaker's feelings. I do both when I sense another's anger or frustration.

There's no other time where a person listens as closely to what you say as when you repeat their words. It's a great tool to diffuse anger, build rapport, and understand the issue for a better solution. Some people tell me, "But Steve, people don't like it when you repeat what they say. You sound like a parrot."

I disagree.

When customers are frustrated to the point of escalation, they feel ecstatic that you took the time to understand their problem and then asked for their confirmation. Understanding people's problems calms people. You also give them confidence in your problem-solving skills.

How do you feel when someone takes the time to SHOW you that they understand your problem(s)? And then asks for your confirmation? E.g., "Correct?"

It feels great!

Why? Because your brain just got a hit of dopamine when the tension was released. How often do people show understanding of our problems? Rarely. After I confirm with words like "correct?" or "right?", I will hear people exhale as they say, "Yes." I've had external customers tell me, "You're the first person at your company that took the time to understand my problem."

Acknowledging and understanding a complaint are a great one-two combination that sets you up for the final step: Solve. If you take the time to do these first two steps, many customers will apologize for their angry outbursts. Acknowledging and understanding the problem are the difficult parts of AUSE as you are still defining the issue, but once it's defined, the solution is relatively easy.

Step 3: S = Solve

At this stage, you will have to regain control and probe to get details of the issue.

The key to offering solutions is to speak with confidence that you WILL solve the problem. You need to own the problem, provided the problem is justified. The reason the customer is upset could be due to other people letting his or her problem go unresolved. Unresolved problems fester. A phrase that I like at the solution stage is, "*I guarantee...*"

What do you do if another problem that wasn't disclosed earlier suddenly pops up?

You restart the AUSE model.

1. Acknowledge what the customer says.

2. Understand the facts and feelings + confirm.

3. Solve it.

Here are strong words to show that you will regain control and solve the problem (provided the customer's issue is justified):

Strong words	Comments
"I will"	Avoid saying, "I'll try", "Maybe I can...", "Hopefully I can...", or other 'words of doubt' that make you sound powerless. If the other party doubts you, s/he may ask for someone else.

"Concern", "issue", "matter", "situation"	I avoid using the word "problem" to turn the heat down. I like to make the issue sound smaller, although some customers will say, "This isn't a concern. It's a major problem." If so, I use the word "problem."
"Easy"	It's a good word as we all want life to be easier. E.g., *"It's easy for me to solve this issue, I'll do....by* (date) *and you will do..., OK?"*
"Help"	This is a wonderful word to use on angry people. Imagine that person is a drowning swimmer. What word do they shout?"
"OK?", "What do you think?"	Involve the other party in the solution you propose.

☝ Solve Tips:

- Don't skip the solution stage. I have heard people acknowledge the customer's problem, even shown understanding and empathy, then change the subject to avoid the solution. Customers will re-ignite.

- Avoid using a 'schoolteacher' explanation style. If you want to educate the person on the correct process, do it subtly and politely. Sometimes, I'll say how I was also confused when I initially saw that process. Most of us have had bad past school experiences and we don't like being lectured to — but we do like being informed. Provide the solution like an adult speaking to another adult. Not as a teacher lecturing a slow child.

- Sometimes it's useful to 'tai chi' the solution back to the other party. E.g., *"What do you suggest we do to solve this matter?"* Or *"So, what do you recommend should be the next steps?"* It involves the other party and leads to a better, and followed, solution.

- Recognize that you can't solve all problems. However, sometimes just the act of acknowledging, understanding, and empathizing solves part of the problem. And that will be enough for some people.

E = Empathize

When people are frustrated or angry, the AUSE model falls flat without empathy. Empathy is the oil in this dispute resolution engine. It shows you care; your tone is important if you want to sound credible. My favorite word to show empathy is "**sorry**."

> … consumers with complaints are looking for more than just refunds. Only 43% said they were satisfied with just a financial solution; 50% said they enjoyed a remedy that involved empathy, an apology or other outcomes unrelated to money; and 60% said they were more satisfied when they received both.[33]

> **Tip:**
>
> If customers refuse to speak with your team members and only want to speak with you, guess what one word they'll expect you to say over and over? They want to speak with you because your team members didn't show empathy. And because they didn't say 'sorry' once, you now need to say it many, many times. Tell your team that it's OK to say, "sorry."

In my experience, saying 'sorry' at the acknowledgment stage, when the customer is red hot, works best. Throwing empathy is like throwing water on a fire. I do it sooner rather than later. It's difficult for people to remain angry once they hear that word.

Some bosses say, "But Steve, I don't like to say 'sorry' as it can be used against me for agreeing that we made a mistake."

I disagree.

---

[33]   Ann-Marie Alcantara, "Customer Complaints, and Their Ways of Complaining, are on the Rise," *Wall Street Journal,* June 14, 2020, https://www.wsj.com/articles/customer-complaints-and-their-ways-of-complaining-are-on-the-rise-11591998939 (Accessed January 7, 2021).

Saying "sorry" shows empathy. It doesn't show agreement. E.g., *"I'm sorry that you feel my staff was disrespectful to you."* This statement doesn't show that you agree with them.

Full AUSE Example

Imagine that Peter, one of your internal customers and a peer, telephones you because he is angry that your team member forgot to send Report A to him as she promised. You investigated and you determined it was your team member's fault.

Step 1: Acknowledge: (Steve listens and shows empathy while Peter speaks)

Peter the Peer	"Steve, I'm upset with your staff, Jill. She promised us she'd send Report A by 5:00 pm yesterday and she still hasn't sent it. We had a meeting with our General Manager and we weren't able to give him all the details about Project X. I looked stupid."
Steve the Supervisor	(Note: while Peter is venting, Steve throws a 'sorry' here and there and an 'Oh, my' or two. Once Peter stops venting, Steve goes to Step 2: Understand).

Step 2: Understand:

Steve the Supervisor	*"Peter, let me see if I understand you. We promised Report A by 5:00 p.m. yesterday and you didn't get it. And because of that your side felt frustrated dealing with the GM because you couldn't answer all his questions on Project X, is that right?"* (Note: to diffuse the situation and maintain Peter's self-esteem, I didn't repeat the negative emotional word: 'stupid').
Peter the Peer	"Yes."

Step 3: Solve:

Steve the Supervisor	*"Again Peter, I'm sorry. Let me suggest that I have my staff email the report to your team member now. I'll have her cc you and me. And for the next six months, I'll have her cc me this report to ensure this process is fixed. I'll also contact the GM and explain to him that it was my department's fault.* *"Are these solutions OK with you?"*
Peter the Peer	Thanks Steve. That's fine. Thanks for offering to call the GM, but it's OK. I'll handle it.
Steve the Supervisor	*"Thanks for highlighting this matter, Peter. Again, my apologies. Take care, buddy. Bye."*

Note: Steve the Supervisor shielded his staff, Jill, by avoiding using her name.

Final Point About Handling Angry Interactions

AUSE focuses on the other angry party. But let's be honest, we cause many angry situations ourselves. I have a temper. Whenever I have allowed my temper to show, it nearly always has damaged a relationship. I may feel good at the time, but I pay a much heavier price later. I have damaged and ruined relationships at all organizational levels.

Human egos are easily damaged; anger is a great way to do that. Your worth at your organization is the sum total of your knowledge, skills, attitude, AND relationships. When you damage your relationships, you are damaging yourself. Keep your anger in check because, if you don't, you will surely lose.

Firing Poor Performers

Firing poor performers is easy. But, as earlier stated, before firing a poor performer you need to determine if it is a 'skill' or 'will' problem and give the person the required resources to improve performance. You've got to be fair and the employee shouldn't be shocked when s/he is fired. Remember the 'enemy' when firing an employee isn't the employee, but the poor performance.

As a new supervisor, I felt bad firing staff. I didn't want to be heartless. I also realized they needed the paycheck because why else were they at work?

But I have since discovered that firing, although unpleasant at the time, can turn into something good. You lose a poor performer; they leave a job that was ill-suited to them. Now, both parties have a better chance to succeed and be happier.

My father had a friend who owned an industrial-sized chicken processing plant. He asked my dad's help to discover who was allowing rotten chickens to go down the processing line and getting consumers sick. A rotten chicken usually has a light green shade to it. There were eight Quality Assurance (QA) inspectors who worked various shifts. The owner believed it had to be one of them.

My dad, an ophthalmologist, went to quick work. He took some dead, plucked chickens and dipped them in green dye. He then slyly placed them intermittently on the conveyor belt to test the various QA inspectors' eyesight. All the inspectors removed the green chickens whenever they passed by, except one. My dad ran more green chickens down the belt again for that particular QA inspector. Again, he allowed them to pass. When my dad asked him why he allowed green chickens to go down the conveyor line, the inspector said, "Because I'm color blind."

My dad asked, "How long have you been working in QA here?"

He replied, "Ten years."

"Why are you doing a job that you can't do?"

He replied, "Because I need the money."

If you have suffered from chicken poisoning in the 1970s in the U.S., it may have been caused by this guy. Anyway, this 'inspector' was immediately fired because the owner had asked the QA team about the quality problem and no one said anything. I don't know what this person next job was, but I'm sure he performed better in it than his previous one.

Stories: The Importance of Networking with Your HR People

Many hiring mistakes are caused by faulty HR processes. HR won't understand your department's unique requirements as well as you. You need to alert HR on your exact requirements as their mistakes will impact your team's performance and success.

 Story 1: At one organization, our HR department's number one criterion to hire a person for my call center was that s/he had to have a secondary school diploma. My number one criterion was s/he had to have good communication skills. HR rejected great people that I interviewed because they lacked a diploma. And I rejected their preferred candidates because they demonstrated poor communication skills.

 Story 2: In one consultancy project at an airport, our task was to increase passengers' customer satisfaction ratings after they dealt with the information counter staff. The client wanted their employees to not only be friendlier at the counters, but also to roam outside the counters to proactively assist people. Unfortunately, the employees were resistant to the imperative of being friendlier and more proactive. A group of them even said, "Why should we be nice to them? They should be nice to us because we're helping them."

When we shared their resistance with HR, we discovered that each employee took a personality test before being hired. We discovered that 80% of the customer-facing staff tested as introverts. Most of them felt uncomfortable being nice to strangers, especially when it came to proactively walking away from the counter and starting up cold conversations. We worked with HR to prevent future hiring mistakes and to transfer many of the counter staff to back-end jobs they felt more comfortable doing.

It's important to show some empathy when firing a poor performer — but avoid showing too much as you don't want the firing to become a cryfest.

You also want to ensure you have other matters in place before the firing like:

- Boxes, if they have to pack up their desk.

- Security for any ex-employee over-reactions.

- Escort process from the office.

- HR support for any final paperwork the ex-employee needs to sign, be given, or things the ex-employee needs to return.

- Timeline they can take to leave the office.

I recommend doing the firing at the start of the day to avoid wasting their time. Do it privately, but don't fire them in your office as they might not leave and now, you're trapped. Do it in a meeting room, their former office, an empty break room, empty pantry, maybe even outside.

So, let's say you need to fire Prem because he's a poor performer. You have given him plenty of coaching and warnings. HR has also approved the firing.

Steve (supervisor)	"Prem, I'm sorry to tell you this. Due to your performance, you're fired. Please pack your desk and leave the building within the hour. Thanks."
Zainal	"But boss, why?"
Steve	"Prem, I'm sorry. Please pack your things. Goodbye."

If Prem continues to ask 'why?', I'll continue to tell him to please pack and leave. I don't want to say anything that can be used against me or the company in a potential labor dispute. Prem has been warned earlier. I told him it was due to his performance. He knows.

Retrenchments

These are more difficult as sometimes the people you retrench are top performers. I have been retrenched and I know how it feels. I was in shock. My Alaskan bank branch had been one of our organization's most profitable branches for years. But when a recession hit, they decided to close us.

I'll never forget the scene. A senior executive flew up from the state of Utah. He stood in front of us. The twenty of us were sitting at our desks in the large work area. The executive twirled two large coins in his hand as he spoke. He reminded me of Captain Bligh from the movie, *Mutiny on the Bounty* (1962).

He said, "Ladies and gentlemen, we've decided to close your branch in the next year due to cost-cutting measures. You'll be given severance pay. Any questions?"

I will never forget three things about his technique:

1. It was fast. I liked that.

2. It was without empathy. I didn't like that.

3. He twirled two coins in his hands. I didn't like that (I felt like I was one of the coins!).

But it did teach me to fire people quickly. There's no need to make it a death by a thousand cuts. People deserve to be told the 'what' and the 'why.'

My retrenchment was the best thing that ever happened to me. It changed my career path from banking to telecommunications, teaching, and HR. I travelled the world for 1.5 years. I can speak French, a bit of Polish and some Malay.

Then, a decade later, at a Malaysian employer, I found myself on an HR retrenchment committee. Our company needed to retrench 300 employees due to a recession. Every day the committee organized the upcoming retrenchment's processes and systems. We wanted to ensure everything was ready on that day like: boxes, retrenchment letters, severance packages, job referral service, press releases, legality, counselling, etc.

We conducted training sessions beforehand for supervisors — on how to retrench their staff and how to handle conflict. We also provided supervisors with a Q&A to help them through this difficult exercise.

Then came the retrenchment day.

Although many employees anticipated the retrenchments, more did not. I had to retrench a good performer that I will never forget.

Early in the morning I called Ms. Gan into a private meeting room.

Steve (supervisor)	"Gan, I'm sorry. You've been retrenched because of the recession."
Gan	"But why me?"
Steve	"I'm sorry—because of the recession."

She asked another why, but I just repeated, "Because of the recession." I didn't want to expose the company to any legal action about her retrenchment. I also don't want to hurt people's egos if they feel slighted for any reason. Why give them something to argue about?

Gan left the building carrying her box. I felt sorry for her. She was a good employee, but that's life. I don't rush good people out of the office when they are retrenched. They should be allowed the time and dignity to say their goodbyes. Still, you don't want them walking around the department hours after they have been retrenched.

Later, I discovered that Gan returned to her love of designing electrical fixtures. She took a job overseas and began earning three times her Malaysian salary.

Of course, some retrenchments don't go smoothly. You have to prepare for those. At our retrenchment, some employees had to be escorted out of the building. One brought his wife and they both shouted loudly that it wasn't fair. The press also attacked the company.

After the initial retrenchment, as part of the HR team, I was assigned to the job counseling center. I helped the retrenched ex-staff write and print their resumes in English. The ex-employees could treat the job center as their own office for three months, with free access to the center's PCs, printers, and online learning materials.

I'll never forget a retrenched field technician who entered. He was my age. He had a few kids. He was an introvert (an 'owl'). He was the type of worker who focused on his job and not office gossip and politics. He was caught completely by surprise. He cried. I didn't know what else to do but say, "I'm sorry."

Our employer nearly went bust, but in the next two to three years, as the economy improved, our organization offered most of the retrenched staff new jobs. About half took the offer, including the technician. When we next saw each other at work, he acted as if he didn't recognize me. I don't know if it was due to embarrassment or if he was in shock when we first met and simply forgot me.

Nowadays, companies are retrenching "our most important assets" by WhatsApp, SMS, email, or other immature methods. This is cowardly and unethical. The retrenched person deserves to be retrenched face-to-face (either in-person or via video). Be courageous and ethical.

Bosses: Be ready to do this more often post-COVID as organizations cut costs to maintain adequate cash levels.

Working for a Bad Boss

From the ages of 12 to 61, I've had over 40 jobs with countless bosses. Early jobs included paperboy, gardener, car wash attendant, guard, babysitter, food server, laborer, summer camp counselor, tutor, busboy, dishwasher, salmon processor, crab griller, zookeeper, and chemical factory worker.

Other jobs included: salesperson, credit analyst, bill collector, English teacher, newspaper columnist, banker, corporate trainer, training manager, contact center manager, consultant, and company president. Of my 40+ bosses, only two were truly horrible. Many more were good and memorable.

I'm happy to say that I've never been fired, though I've come close a couple times.

Before labeling someone a 'bad boss', you first need to inspect yourself. Are you a bad employee? I've had colleagues who labeled good and great bosses 'bad'. I asked one colleague why he was quitting. He said, "Steve, my boss doesn't develop me."

"What do you mean?"

He said, "He doesn't give me the training I need."

"Have you told him?"

He replied, "No, he should know."

I disagree.

Bosses aren't all-knowing mind readers. If you need training and your boss doesn't see it, you have to highlight it. Bosses are fallible humans and they need your help to be a good boss. If you don't highlight operational issues, then you're just as 'bad' as s/he is. You lack courage. You may even be worse than the boss because you see something that the boss doesn't.

As we saw in Chapter 4 on communications, just because your boss doesn't think like you, it doesn't mean s/he is 'bad'. S/he is just different and likely thinks in a different 'silo' from yours. You will need to adapt to theirs.

That doesn't mean there are no bad bosses. There are. Bad bosses cause an enormous amount of stress. They will damage your health and career. A bad job with a good boss is easier to swallow than a good job with a bad boss.

Bad bosses damage your career by:

- Claiming credit for themselves.
- Pushing blame to you.
- Not sharing their expertise to develop you.
- Not being fair and not creating a performance-based work culture.
- Not supporting you in the organization either by defending you from superiors or ensuring you have enough resources to achieve your departmental goals.
- Not promoting you because they feel threatened by you.
- Not developing you with new knowledge, skills, special projects, training, conferences, etc.
- Not enhancing your organizational visibility to increase your organizational value.

I'm sure the list is longer, but I'm stopping now because it brings back too many bad memories. So, what do you do if you have a bad boss? You may like your job and team members, but if your boss won't help you succeed, then you won't succeed. Is working for him or her worthwhile?

Bad bosses are one of the top reasons people leave organizations. When working for any boss you need a 'Plan B' exit strategy as nothing is guaranteed in business. But when you work for a bad boss, you need a 'Plan BB' (Bad Boss) and its timeline is shorter.

Here are some Plan BBs if you have communicated your concerns with him or her and it still doesn't work:

- Build a network of senior management supporters in your organization. Ask them for advice. If they like you, ask them for a job in their departments. Note: Don't share your bad boss problem with a peer as it can hurt you later.

- Find a senior mentor. Again, s/he can advise you and maybe use his or her senior organizational contacts to fix your bad boss situation.

- Take courses or training in other skills that you enjoy, then consider an interdepartmental transfer.

- Look for another job outside if you can't transfer because you are just wasting your time. Career advisors recommend that the #1 factor to use to evaluate job offers is: "Who will be my new boss?" If you have a good boss, your chances of achieving your personal and corporate goals are much higher as good bosses increase your organizational visibility.

- Alert HR if you have evidence of your bad boss's consistent unfair treatment. Be forewarned that this is a dangerous step, but if your bad boss has a bad history with them, they may be receptive to hear about it. Don't go to HR without your facts because you could be considered a troublemaker and be asked to leave. At one of my past organizations, a middle manager was accused of sexual harassment by a young, female team member. HR investigated her complaint and found other cases of his odd behavior among young women, but none of the other women ever filed formal complaints. In addition, his boss, a senior leader, protected him. Although HR believed the young woman, they didn't act due to lack of hard evidence. The young woman kept her job, but she was assigned to a different boss. The middle-manager eventually became a senior leader.

This chapter shared many kinds of supervisory problems, and you will have plenty more during your career. This book can't cover them all, but I hope you will have a better chance of tackling them when they do occur with the ideas I have shared.

Some problems will cause you and your team stress. It's important when others are losing their cool that you maintain yours. People in crisis situations look to leaders for strength and guidance. Stay cool and lead. Panic helps no one. Don't be afraid to decide!

My Chapter's Key Points:

- Complaints and problems are part of the supervisor's job. You will get plenty of them. If there were none, you wouldn't have a job.

- Many interpersonal complaints or conflicts can be solved with proper communication skills.

- A leader who can't decide isn't a leader.

- The Two-Lenses technique is a tool to help you make decisions:

  1st Lens: What is the overall benefit of the decision? Greatest good for the greatest number.

  2nd Lens: Can I explain and defend the decision well?

- For internal and external customer complaints about my team, I use the 3-step AUSE model:

  1. Acknowledge: Show the other party you are listening

  2. Understand: Show that you listened by repeating the issue's facts and by acknowledging the speaker's feelings.

  3. Solve: Show the other party that you are serious about solving it. Speak confidently by using strong words like, "I will…"

     - Empathize: This isn't a step, but it's mostly just one word: 'sorry'. It's a lovely word that calms angry people.

- Firing poor performers helps your company, you, and them. Poor performance cause headaches and deal with it before it becomes a migraine. If performance doesn't improve after the necessary coaching, resources, or training; you need to get that person 'off the bus.' When you fire people, do it privately, quickly, and with some (but not too much) empathy. Remember: poor performers aren't bad; their performance is bad.

- Retrenching staff is difficult but sometimes necessary. Do it privately, quickly, and with some (but not too much) empathy.

- Before labeling someone a 'bad boss', look at yourself. Are you a bad employee?

- Bad bosses are dangerous to your career. Take action! First, try communicating with him or her. If that doesn't work, consider a Plan BB.

  Ideas include:

  - Speaking with your senior management contacts for advice.

  - Transferring.

  - Continuing your education and possibly changing careers.

  - Quitting.

  - Alerting HR — but be prepared with evidence if you go this route.

> As you strengthen your leadership skills, you become more valuable. The next short chapter talks about your future career.

CHAPTER 8:

PREPARING FOR YOUR NEXT ACT

What you do today can improve all your tomorrows
— Ralph Marston, professional American football player

This book's goal was to give you the tools to excel not only with your team, but also with your peers, your boss, senior management, members of the board, and key customers. I want you to achieve great results and receive the recognition you deserve to advance in your career. Pre-COVID, the road to promotion was easier to understand, but now the world has changed.

COVID has changed our jobs and work environments. We have long dreamed of the future job where everyone is connected, and where work can be done anywhere. We knew this would happen, but we didn't think it would happen so soon. Now we live in a broadband society with ever faster capabilities. Employers will take advantages of these improvements in high-speed infrastructure to change the way we work.

Although I'm writing this book during the pandemic, we can already see certain COVID shifts that will change people's jobs.

These include:

1. Increasing usage of automation, IT, apps, and robots to lower business expenses. Plus these systems and machines don't get sick.

2. Cash is king. Cash generating products, services, lines-of-business, and departments take precedence. Additionally, businesses will re-think their office space rental requirements to save even more cash.

3. Increasing usage of remote-based work. Most employees like WFH's freedom and timesaving qualities; businesses enjoy reduced expenses. Plus, remote-based work is more climate friendly as it reduces road traffic, air pollution, and paper consumption.

4. Top performers (aka 'essential workers') will be valued more. They were the ones who saved the company during COVID. There will be a talent war for them.

5. The importance of having good communication and teamworking skills will increase in our rapidly changing future. We will be like military kids who change schools every few years and need to make new friends and school contacts quickly. Except we will need to upgrade our skills and be able to work with all types of people in all types of new project teams.

Job Hopping Pays

If you are a top performer (with evidence that proves this) and your boss or organization doesn't value you, consider working elsewhere. Job hopping pays. A recent article in *Forbes* discussed the benefits of job hopping (every three years or so) in different industries:

> According to an analysis of the data by *Bloomberg*, the biggest beneficiaries are job hoppers in the information industry who realized 9.7% annual wage growth, construction workers with an 8.7% increase, and professional and business services with an 8.3% premium.

Those who stayed at their companies earned about a 4% increase in pay. On average, those who choose to switch jobs enjoyed compensation growth of 5.3%. The only large groups that suffered from falling wages—when changing jobs—were in the leisure and hospitality sectors...[34]

Banker story 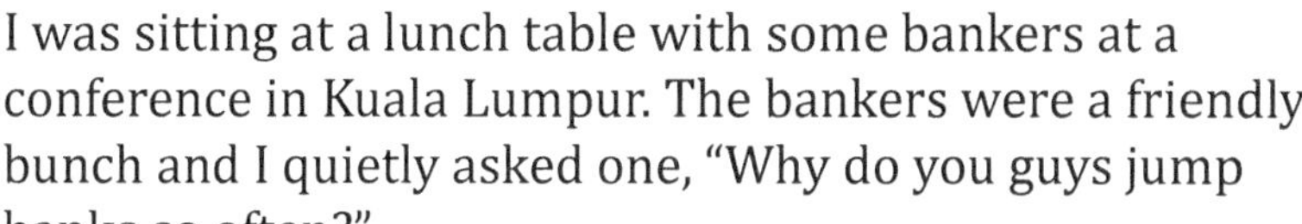

I was sitting at a lunch table with some bankers at a conference in Kuala Lumpur. The bankers were a friendly bunch and I quietly asked one, "Why do you guys jump banks so often?"

He replied, "It's the only way we can make money." He said that if he stayed at one bank, he'd get a small annual increment. But if he jumped to another bank, he'd get a big pay boost. Jumping pays.

Whether you decide to job hop or not depends on you, but in any event, you still need to increase your organizational value to prove your worth.

9 Ways to Increase Your Organizational (and Industry) Value.

1. Continually Grow Your Organizational Network

As stated throughout this book, your relationships with peers, superiors, key customers, and even competitors are key to succeed in any organization. Post-COVID, more effort will be needed to communicate with your network, especially if you or they work remotely.

If you work remotely, alert your boss that you still want to be involved in key meetings and decisions. Don't go *'out of sight; out of mind.'* Update your boss on your career goals, especially if they have changed post-COVID. Update superiors frequently about your successes. Ask your boss what else you can do to help him or her achieve more. Proactively warn

34   Jack Kelly, "A New Study Concludes That It Literally Pays to Switch Jobs Right Now," *Forbes,* July 26, 2019, https://www.forbes.com/sites/jackkelly/2019/07/26/a-new-study-concludes-that-it-literally-pays-to-switch-jobs-right-now/#79a9a4c95959 (Accessed June 6, 2020).

your boss on impending unpleasant outcomes versus giving nasty surprises later.

2. Take Lateral and Promotional Transfers:

Transfers develop new skills and broaden your organizational network. Transfers allowed me to leave my organization and start my own company. At one employer, I faced the brutal truth that my career had stagnated. It seemed that for every year I worked there, it was just another year of doing the same job. I was in a time loop and I wasn't developing.

I decided that I needed to gain new skills. I asked my boss for a lateral transfer to a different department. My teammates, peers, and friends thought I was crazy. In Malaysia, maintaining 'face' is important. Here, lateral transfers are considered bad whereas promotional transfers are viewed positively. But that wasn't important to me. I just wanted the opportunity to gain new skills, broaden my organizational network, and meet more industry contacts. In addition, my new boss (a member of senior management) was also a friend who would increase my organizational visibility.

The lateral transfer was a success. I achieved everything I had hoped for and more.

If you don't want to transfer to other departments, then consider transferring within your department. Let's say you are a telecom radio frequency (RF) engineer in the RF Department. You understand RF technology and you are great at it. Perhaps it's time to try something different to broaden your skill set like in tower construction, field operations, or switching? The highest-paid engineers that I know take their engineering knowledge and move into sales and marketing. There, they begin to sell to large corporate clients. They gain new non-technical and business skills and contacts that complement their existing technical knowledge and contacts. Their versatility (demonstrated and achieved by moving between the technical and non-technical worlds) makes them special. And when you're special, you're valuable, and when you're valuable, you're paid more. You're also the last to be retrenched.

If I had to re-do my employee working years, I'd wish I had taken more transfers. I have experience in Sales, Credit /Collections, HR Training, and Education. I wished I had done a stint in HR Staffing and Recruitment, Fraud Management, and many others. It would have made me even more multi-skilled. The best and cheapest training you can ever get is on-the-job training with your current employer. You even get paid for it!

With the increase in IT, AI, robotics, cloud computing, and other technologies, being flexible is more important than ever. "Job security" is extinct. The percent of workers in the gig economy will only increase. Organizations face too much regulatory and economic risk to offer lots of people permanent jobs, especially post-COVID.

One of my former employers, a wireless phone company, closed a 900+ seat call center in Phoenix, Arizona. COVID-19 has convinced them that the cost of operating such a facility in the desert — with air-conditioning and 700 parking spots — is just not worthwhile. These large-office-based jobs will be lost forever. Their employees now take customer calls from home. The company saves too much money. Who wouldn't want to avoid that kind of expense?

When it comes to getting, saving, or making money, humans act fast. If you don't believe me, throw some dollar bills on the floor and see how fast people scramble for them. That's life. That's business. The quickest, most adaptable people survive.

You need to make yourself as valuable as you can to survive these competitive times. With increased remote-based work, the trend is towards ROVE (Results-Only-Work-Environment)[35] jobs, where employees and their managers focus more on the work output than how the work is done. Your challenge here is setting the right KPIs (Key Performance In-

---

35 Jodi Thompson and Cali Ressler coined the term 'ROVE'. See https:// https://www.gorowe.com (Accessed June 21, 2020).

dicators) and monitoring systems to ensure your team is actually working.

3. Volunteer for Special Projects

Special projects increase your organizational visibility, especially when you're successful. They do cause you added pressure, but pressure is good. Run towards pressure because if you can conquer it, you will acclimatize yourself to handle more pressure. And you will receive greater and greater responsibilities.

You have put in enormous effort at school, work, and in training to develop valuable skills, knowledge, and an organizational network to reach that point in your career to receive that gift of pressure. Not everyone gets to receive it. Others long for it and never get the opportunity. You are blessed. As the NBA basketball coach Doc Rivers says, *"Pressure is a privilege."*

4. Ensure Greater Job Security By Becoming the Best Possible Boss You Can Be

Since lifetime corporate employment is virtually extinct, work is becoming more transactional and lasts only for as long as it's beneficial for both parties. It can be terminated with little advance notice.

Writing about today's job insecurity, Adzhar Ibrahim, an ex-chief HR officer at three listed Malaysian companies, advises:

> Companies too discovered 'shareholder value' which basically meant high share prices no matter what. Employees had become disposable. Jack Welch, GE's CEO in the 80's, became known as 'Neutron Jack', after the atomic bomb that kills people whilst leaving buildings intact. He delivered loads of 'shareholder value' ... and unemployment.

> I advise employees instead to be loyal to their jobs. Be the best accountant or engineer there is – be competent and productive, and live the company's values and

expectations. Then if one day the company says, 'sorry bub, you're out-- shareholders' value you know', you'd still have your own competence, track record, and confidence in yourself. [36]

5. Gain Your Competitor's Respect and Camaraderie

Your greatest chance of getting a large salary boost is when you are 'pinched' by the competition. Don't make your competitors your enemies. They're your friends because one day they may offer you a better opportunity than your existing organization ever will. In any industry, you will see people jumping between companies within that industry. Each time they jump, they receive more money. Sometimes they even jump back to the original employer for a higher salary and position. Good people with a strong industry network are valued anywhere.

6. Further Your Education:

On weekends, I attended a local university to get a master's in education for Instructional Technology. It was painful losing my weekends and hitting the books, but after a few months the new behavior became like second nature. Then, when school ended two years later, it felt odd having free weekends.

School also broadened my external network. One fellow student (and friend) has resulted in an enormous amount of business for both of us. Great to have met you, Jude Louis!

Education isn't limited to physical schools. Nowadays there are countless free and reputable online courses as well. COVID has made online learning even more popular.

Educationists say the knowledge we gain in our formal education has a shelf-life of ten years. Like an arms race, we are in a skill race to constantly upskill ourselves. To survive, bad bosses must become good bosses. Good bosses must become better bosses. The struggle to improve never ends.

36   Adzhar Ibrahim, comments on *LinkedIn*, July 2, 2020, https://www.linkedin.com/feed/update/urn:li:activity:6684379186574061568/?commentUrn=urn%3Ali%3Acomment%3A(activity%3A6684109824579518464%2C6684379156983242752) (Accessed July 2, 2020).

7. Attend as Many External Training Events, Conferences, and Industry Meets as You Can:

As a boss, we're usually too busy putting out fires to focus on our own learning and development. That's dangerous. External learning events allow you to learn new ideas while increasing the value of your industry network.

> **Tip:**
>
> Become a speaker at industry conferences to gain extra exposure and recognition.

8. Write for Your Industry's Magazines, Newspapers, and Websites (Including LinkedIn groups):

Again, this builds your industry exposure, enriches your network, and increases your recognition. That's why I wrote my first book: *Debt Collections: Stir-Fried or Deep-Fried?* (2007).

9. Read Books:

Reading books is tough in the age of the internet and social media, but reading is a cheap way to gain loads of knowledge and ideas. If you interview the most successful CEOs, nearly all of them are voracious readers. Assume that every book's writer has at least ten years of experience, then multiply that by the number of practical books you read. How many centuries of wisdom, tips, and advice can you get in just one year?

> **Tip:**
>
> Give good business books to your Stars. It's a special way to connect and develop them. Personalize your gift by writing and dating a special message inside (use EEC+).

My Chapter's Key Points:

- Job hopping results in more money for you than staying in one organization.
- You are a boss because management thinks you are good. Now prove it. Develop yourself to become an asset that is worth your salary (and more).
- Increase your organizational and industry value by:
    1. Continually growing your organizational and industry network.
    2. Taking lateral and promotional transfers. It's the best training you can ever get.
    3. Volunteering for special projects.
    4. Becoming loyal to your job to be the best boss you can be.
    5. Gaining respect and comradery from your competitors.
    6. Going back to school to gain new skills, knowledge, and contacts.
    7. Attending external training, conferences, and industry meets to network and learn.
    8. Writing for your industry to raise your visibility.
    9. Reading books.

Parting Words

Thank you for reading *Good Boss, Better Boss.* I pray that you have gained practical tips, models, and knowledge to help you lead others. It took patience, dedication, and a commitment to personal excellence on your part to get through this book. Please continue being an impactful boss by helping your organization and team achieve their results and dreams-- and in doing so—achieve your own.

The rest of the book provides some additional resources for you.

CHAPTER 9

SEVEN COMMON SUPERVISORY QUESTIONS AND ANSWERS

I would rather have questions that can't be answered than answers that can't be questioned.
— Richard Feynman, American physicist

When I conduct supervisory training programs, I get a lot of questions.

Here are the most common:

Q1: How do I supervise someone who was my friend, but now I'm their boss?

A: Tough. They might have even applied for your position. Speak to that person privately and 'tai chi' the issue to him or her. E.g., *"I know we are friends, but now I'm the boss. How do you think we should manage this new situation?"*

By tai chi'ing you show that you're willing to listen to their opinion to resolve it. Before your meeting is over, let your friend know that you are a performance-based, fair supervisor and you expect him or her to do their best. You may want to end with, "I'm happy you're on my team."

But, who knows, you may lose the friendship, such is life. People, even friends, don't like to be told what to do. General George Patton when speaking about his soldiers said, *"I don't want them to love me, I want them to fight for me."*

Q2: How do I supervise older employees with more experience than I have?

A: Be honest. Speak privately with him/her/them.

e.g.,
"I know you have a lot of experience in this company doing this job. And I need your help to share your experience with the juniors and even me. I'm open to any suggestions that you may have as long as they are logical and presented politely. What do you think?"

The key word is **'help.'** People dislike asking for help because they think it shows weakness. Instead, it shows strength and confidence. It's also psychologically difficult for people to refuse requests for help. Use it.

Q3: Should I promote my best performers to be the next supervisors?

A: I support internal promotions, but you still have to be careful. Supervising people has a different skill-set. Do you think your top performer can switch mental tracks to become a boss? Some can, some can't. At one employer, a 'Star' taught me how to collect debts. She had a work style where she'd take no excuses from debtors. She was like the Canadian Mounties, "We always get our man." Except she always got her payment. Due to her stellar performance, she was promoted to supervisor.

She failed miserably.

She had difficulty accepting that her team's skill level wasn't as high as hers. And when they asked her for advice and tips, she got angry because she couldn't understand that they couldn't understand. She lacked patience and was eventually fired.

Q4: What if my organization won't support my desire to implement a fair (ethical) and performance-based system within my team?

A: If you work in government, you may have no choice.

If you work in the corporate sector, leave. If your organization doesn't want to be ethical and performance-based, then its future isn't assured. Eventually it will go bust. Future potential employers could ask, *"Why did you stay at such a corrupt place?"* Find an organization (or start your own) that better reflects your ethics. It will have a better chance of succeeding and you will be happier.

Q5: I don't trust my team. How can I be open to them?

A: You either inherited or hired the wrong people. Perhaps you didn't train them well enough to trust their skills or knowledge. I'm sure they also distrust you. If you want to succeed, you have no choice but to trust them. You're a supervisor, not a dictator, you need their buy-in to achieve and hopefully surpass the target. Start trusting them a little at a time. Ensure you get your Stars on-board first. I suggest you have a team communication session and share the 'what' and the 'why' of an upcoming small, new change that you will take. Celebrate any small wins. Trust takes time. Good luck.

Q6: As a woman, how do I supervise a team full of men?

A: Sometimes it's raining men, so be honest with them. In your first team meeting highlight the 'elephant in the room', *"It looks like I'm your new boss. I promise that I won't let my gender interfere in our success. I know you won't either. My style of managing is performance-based and fair. We are here to get paid to achieve our company's goals. I know you are all professionals and will work hard to accomplish that goal. I also hope we can have fun doing it. What do you think?"*

Q7: What do I do if my boss is always busy?

A: Schedule a time to meet. If s/he is too busy at work, perhaps before work, at lunch, or after work? You need regular face time if you want to succeed and grow in your job. A good boss can develop you, promote you, and give you future job recommendations. It's critical you see him or her at regular intervals. If you have tried all these ideas and your boss is still too busy, sorry, you have a bad boss. A boss's #1 function is to develop their staff to achieve or surpass the organization's results. If your boss doesn't do this, s/he isn't a boss; but possibly a narcissistic psychopath who is more interested in occupying a seat and collecting a paycheck than making an impact on their people. When a bad boss constantly tells you, *"I have no time."* What s/he is really saying is, *"I have no time FOR YOU."*

Find a better boss.

13 GOOD BOSS, BETTER BOSS BEHAVIORS

I will assume that you already possess the good leadership perquisites of courage and ethics. You are now ready to build the right work environment (O/S) to succeed:

1. Performance-based.

2. Fair.

3. Develops the team's creative thinking skills to problem-solve: *"I don't know. What do you think?"*

4. Asks questions and shares an issue's 'what' and 'why' (big picture) to increase meaning in people's work.

5. Highlights problems early versus giving nasty surprises later.

6. Coaches and improves people properly.

7. Shields the team from above.

8. Shares credit, accepts blame.

9. Possesses a sense of humor. There will be times when all you can do is laugh.

10. Continually learns new skills and knowledge to become a better boss.

11. Builds strong organizational and industry networks.

12. Able to make decisions.

13. Chases and welcomes pressure.

20 BAD BOSS BEHAVIORS

1. Gives blame and takes credit.
2. Doesn't coach or does it badly.
3. Possesses the infallible mentality.
4. Doesn't delegate. You are the company's 'bottleneck'.
5. Poor role model.
6. Doesn't display courage and ethics.
7. Unfair. Sets rules with double standards. One for you and one for everyone else.
8. Uses discrimination-based standards e.g., age, race, religion, gender, education, beauty, etc.
9. Manages upwards while neglecting the team.
10. Afraid to decide.
11. Tries to act like a friend to the team and not a boss (Note: being friendly is OK).
12. Acts aloof and doesn't get to know the team.
13. Treats team members as personal servants.
14. Treats team members as machines or robots.
15. Loses cool (or hides) in stressful situations.
16. Heartlessness. No empathy or sense of humor.
17. Lazy. Abdicates responsibility.
18. Steals.
19. Lies.
20. And the worst... disrespects people, especially in public.

EPILOGUE: SHACKLETON'S LESSONS

Sir Ernest Shackleton, the British polar explorer, is a leader who inspires me. I am particularly awed by the courage and ethics he displayed during his failed voyage to the South Pole[37]. On 18 January 1915, his ship, *The Endurance,* became trapped in sea ice. It was abandoned on 27 October. For the next five months, his crew of 28 camped on the ice. On 9 April 1916, the ice began to crack. Shackleton decided that their best chance to survive was to travel in the three, 6.1 m (20') lifeboats to row and sail 557 km (346 miles) to solid ground on Elephant Island.

The five-day journey in rough, freezing seas nearly ended their lives. Concerned that one of his team member's fingers would get frostbite after losing his gloves, he gave Frank Hurley his own mittens. As a result, Shackleton suffered frostbite that would plague him for the rest of his short life.

Elephant Island was a desolate place, hopelessly far from the shipping lanes and any chance of rescue. The men survived by eating penguins and seals while living in a shack made from two of the wooden boats. Shackleton decided their best chance of survival was to take a risky 1,330 km (830 mile) journey to the whaling stations on South Georgia Island.

On 24 April, Shackleton and five others set off in a small boat. He took special care in selecting his five companions.

---

37   Paul Ward, "Sir Ernest Shackleton Endurance Expedition Trans-Antarctica 1914-1917 (Parts 1-4)," *Cool Antarctica,* https://www.coolantarctica.com/Antarctica%20fact%20file/History/Shackleton-Endurance-Trans-Antarctic_expedition.php (Accessed June 20, 2020).

They were chosen for a combination of their skills, knowledge, and attitudes. He chose a carpenter (who disliked him) for his repairing skills, the Endurance's captain for his navigational skills, and two strong rowers who could sometimes display negative attitudes. He didn't want to leave the two (and their negativity) with the rest of the men back on Elephant Island.

During the voyage, they survived a hurricane that sunk a 500-ton steamer ship. They eventually reached the far side of South Georgia island on 10 May, but it took them another ten days to hike to the whaling stations. Luckily, they were able to raise a rescue party for the men back on Elephant Island. The stranded men were rescued after waiting for nearly four and a half months.

The Endurance crew suffered no loss of life.

Historians study how Shackleton's mission, although a failure, succeeded in bringing back all his men alive. They believe it came down primarily to his management techniques. Before the voyage, he received 5,000 applications to be crew members. Shackleton used unorthodox interviewing techniques. He asked odd questions like, "Can you sing?" He knew that there would be boring times and he needed positive people in such work environments. Another crew member was possibly hired for his banjo-playing skills to liven up the workplace. He ensured he got the right people 'on the bus' — 'on the boat' in this case.

Shackleton built a fun work environment and loosened the traditional ship's hierarchy of that era. Chores were distributed equally regardless of rank. There were nightly sing-alongs, jokes, and games. Shackleton socialized with his team and understood each person's personality to learn how to get the best out of him. Although he was frequently depressed about their dire circumstances, he projected a positive attitude at all times.

In *The Worst Journey in the World,* Sir Raymond Priestley aptly distilled the key characteristics of the first generation of Antarctic explorers: "Scott for scientific method, Amundsen for speed and efficiency, but when disaster strikes and all hope is gone, get down on your knees and pray for Shackleton."

To become a better leader or supervisor, you will need the qualities of all three to weather today's stormy seas.

Best of luck in your voyage.

ABOUT THE AUTHOR

I hope you enjoyed this book.

Steve Coyle is a speaker, trainer, author, consultant, and businessman. His training and consultancy company, ServiceWinners International Sdn. Bhd., is available to provide the following services:

- Training on supervisory, credit, collections, customer service, writing, and —

- Coaching

- Train-the-Trainer

- Managing Difficult Conversations

- Handling Hardcore Customers

Steve is an American who is married to a beautiful Malaysian, Choon. They have an active teenage son, Hugh. He has lived in Kuala Lumpur since 1995. He has worked in the banking, retail, education, and telecommunication industries in Alaska and Seattle, and in the Middle East, Poland, and Malaysia.

He and his training team have conducted practical learning programs and consultancy assignments in Singapore, Myanmar, Brunei, India, Cyprus, the United States, and Afghanistan. Now in the COVID age many of these workshops are conducted online.

Steve has an MBA from Gonzaga University (U.S.) and a Masters in Instructional Technology from Universiti Malaya (Malaysia). He is a Certified Credit Executive from the National Association of Credit Management (U.S.) and a Certified Financial Collection Professional (Canada).

If you would like to contact Steve with any questions, comments, or request the free coaching checklist form, send him an email at:

steve@servicewinners.com

Or call:

+60 12 2000 998.

More information about Steve and ServiceWinners can be found at: www.servicewinners.com.

Changing the world, one better boss after another.

Also by Steve...

Debt Collections: Stir-Fried or Deep-Fried?

Asian & Western Strategies to Collect More Money,

Reduce Bad Debts, and Keep More Customers.